The Spirit of Camphill

Karl König with John Jephson, at Murtle House 1953
(Photo by Carlo Pietzner)

The Spirit of Camphill

Birth of a Movement

Karl König

Floris Books

Karl König Archive Publication, Vol. 18
Subject: The Camphill movement
Series editor: Richard Steel

Karl König's collected works are issued by
the Karl König Archive, Aberdeen
in co-operation with the Ita Wegman Institute
for Basic Research into Anthroposophy, Arlesheim

First published in this form by Floris Books in 2018

© 2018 Trustees of the Karl König Archives

All rights reserved. No part of this publication may
be reproduced without the prior permission of
Floris Books, Edinburgh
www.florisbooks.co.uk

MIX
Paper from
responsible sources
FSC® C117931

British Library CIP Data available
ISBN 978-178250-497-9
Printed & bound by MBM Print SCS Ltd, Glasgow

Contents

Introduction *by Richard Steel*	7
Outcasts in Scotland: Pioneers in an Old Manse	41
The Candle on the Hill	47
Three Stars, Pillars and Essentials *by Richard Steel*	72
The Three Stars of the Camphill Movement	90
The Three Pillars of the Camphill Movement	108
The Three Essentials of Camphill	128
The Birth of a Movement	140
Modern Community Building	171
Address to the Tutzinger Stern	178
Appendix	182
Fragments from the story of Camphill 1939–1940 by Anke Weihs	182
W.F. Macmillan and the beginnings of Camphill	205
Karl König's star chart drawing by Alan Thewless	209
Notes of a lecture in Sheffield	212
Letter to Carlo Pietzner	214
The spirit like a dove: the logo of Camphill by Richard Steel	216
Notes and Sources	223
Bibliography	229
Index	231

Editor's note

The texts by Karl König have been edited a little. Some words and phrases used then to describe people with learning difficulties or handicaps are no longer acceptable or even understandable. Often too, it is noticeable that König thought in German while he wrote or spoke in English, so that some phrases have been put into more felicitous English. His quotations of lectures by Steiner, which he often rendered rather freely from the German, have been replaced by the latest published translations.

Unless otherwise noted all pictures are from the Karl König Archive.

Introduction

Background, Becoming and Birth of Camphill
Richard Steel

The Spirit of Camphill – Birth of a Movement – the title already hints that this volume of Karl König's works will not present a history of the Camphill movement which would have to extend onto the present situation and newest developments. Presenting the Camphill movement in the context of Karl König's *works* sends us on an expedition searching for the roots, the inner motifs and the historic setting of the birth process; puts the question of König's biographic situation, of the ideals he felt and perhaps learnt more and more to articulate; of the social context and how he guided this. To understand a birth means to at least include the development from conception. But perhaps above all it is the question of what being, what spirit wishes to realise itself – and be realised – through this birth and becoming.

It is a wonder in itself to observe how Karl König as 'father' of Camphill again and again struggled to grasp the reality of his 'child'– a movement that expanded to more than a hundred communities over four continents within half a century and today has 'seeded out' to influence inner purpose and striving in many people and communities beyond those borders. He wrote down his observations on special occasions – like the tenth anniversary of his flight from a troubled Europe, or on the twenty-first birthday of Camphill; with high esteem for what had been accomplished, with great hopes for the future, but also always with questions and an openness toward a biography in becoming. For some his openness to changing circumstances was a challenge, when he saw the necessity to create new social forms, dissolving old ones to which they had only just adjusted!

This volume presents texts – essays and an address – in which König looked at the evolving movement and went into description of elements that were sometimes not yet even evident for those living in and creating those communities; bringing substantial elements to consciousness, reminding of and re-connecting to the original ideals. This introduction adds content and context out of other important sources such as letters and diaries, but also conversations, meetings in which this development was reviewed and commented. When was Camphill actually born? Where are its roots to be found and what was the original impulse?

Of course the birth of the Camphill movement is very closely tied to the biography of Karl König. In the introductory essay for the volume *Becoming Human: A Social Task* we have already outlined the evolving of König's social impulse. Here it becomes clear how closely König saw his task in connection to the central aims of anthroposophy itself. It belonged very much to his deepest concerns that this central mission of Rudolf Steiner – to imbue social reality with esoteric wisdom – was not able to unfold as it would need to, particularly through the political situation, destroying the spiritual roots of Central Europe altogether, but also through the internal problems of the Anthroposophical Society itself, which also affected him and his mentor, Ita Wegman directly.[1] In 1949 König was able to give a lecture at the Goetheanum in Dornach for the first time since the war. He spoke about Camphill. We know from his notes that he placed Camphill into the history of curative education, describing this similarly to the way he wrote later for the essay 'Mignon, The History of Curative Education,' which was first published in 1950, but we now know that he had planned this already in 1945.[2] The notes for his 1949 lecture show that he intended to tell about two 'streams' – the outer and the inner foundations of Camphill. They end with the lines:

This report – a small grain out of the gratitude owed to Rudolf Steiner.
The Goetheanum could become an altar of gratitude.[3]

One birth moment

The deep questions König experienced in his youth already and his strong will to give his life to healing for humanity, resonated strongly with his first experiences of Rudolf Steiner's intentions. But it was the deepest question about the origin and development of the human being that not only led him to the Embryological Institute in Vienna, but then through his studies to Ita Wegman, with whom Steiner had begun the anthroposophical medical movement. Through her König could link to the individuality of Rudolf Steiner more deeply and find his feelings verified, that the medical task of healing must be seen in close connection to the healing necessary in social life, in society. Soon he could experience how this connection was enhanced by the tasks of curative education, setting him on the path to Pilgramshain and subsequently to Camphill.

Originating in his contemplations on embryology, the motif of the descending spirit being, which König soon saw in the image of the dove, is something we will turn to in various ways, as it accompanied König throughout his life and became, in the true sense of the word, symbolic for the mission of the Camphill movement. The realisation that struck him on his first visit to an Advent garden in Ita Wegman's curative institute, the Sonnenhof became one of those moments that we can call an element of birth, or perhaps of conception, for Camphill. In this context the text needs to sound, that is to be found in the essay 'Candle on the Hill':

But now I saw myself sitting in a circle with my children and their helpers. In the centre of the room there was a little mound built up of earth and covered with moss and on top of it stood a large burning candle. Around the mound, a spiral of moss had been laid out, reaching far into the room; it almost touched the circle of children. Each child, holding in its hand an apple into which a small candle was fixed, had to walk along the spiral to light its own candle at the central candle on the hill ...

My own heart flowed over with compassion. I saw these severely handicapped beings who appeared so happy and bright. I suddenly and profoundly experienced that the spark of the living spirit was present in each one of them in spite of their disabilities.

And in this hour, the decision was taken that I would dedicate my life to the care and education of these children. It was a promise I gave myself: to build a hill upon which a big candle was to burn so that many children, infirm and with handicaps, would be able to find their way to this beacon of hope and to light their own candles so that each single flame would be able to radiate and shine forth.

At this moment I did not know that the hill would in time bear the name Camp-hill. An ideal started to grow in my mind and heart.

Indeed the essay, which König wrote for the twenty-first birthday of Camphill in 1961, received its title from this very experience and from the sense of fulfilment he must have gained seeing the way he was guided to this very spot named Camphill – a hill with a very special history of its own.

This very geographic place that his group of pioneers were 'by chance' led to in 1940, seemed to verify the connection of this humble beginning with historic threads of social and religious impulses: it had been stewarded by the last members of

INTRODUCTION

the Order of the Temple – the Knights Templar. Piece by piece a higher destiny seemed to be revealing itself. Through their journey of exile to Scotland this group of knights had escaped the persecution their movement was deemed to, being persecuted and tortured, the last Grand Master burned at the stake on March 11, 1314 in Paris.[4]

With the move to Camphill House König began looking into the history of the Templars and what Rudolf Steiner had indicated about them. It must have been a revelation to him when he found that Steiner stressed the importance of the Templars, looking beyond their historic significance to the deeper spiritual meaning of their tasks. Steiner spoke of this quite centrally in lectures about the development of Europe between east and west, between positive spirituality that lived in the Idealists and Romantics of the eighteenth and nineteenth centuries, and the forces of evil and retardation of society's progress. Soon after this König gave his friends and closest co-workers the central kernel of these lectures as the leading thought – which still stands today – of the Camphill Community. Reading through these remarkable lectures that Rudolf Steiner gave in the midst of the First World War, one can have the impression that these lines really stand out within the lecture, as if Rudolf Steiner was perhaps quoting something, changing the mood to something almost like a prayer. It is these lines that König, with his uncanny sense for the essential, took as the kernel.

> Increasingly the longing arose for the complete Christianising of the treasures of cosmic wisdom and of earth's evolution, and for the complete Christianising of earthly life – a Christianising of earthly life in such a way that the suffering of the earth, the pain of the earth and the sorrow of the earth appear as the cross of the earth which finds its comfort, its elevation and its redemption in the Rose Symbol of the Crucifix.
> There were people who were again and again inspired

by this symbol, in whom what was meant to be killed with the burning of the Knights Templar lived on. In these inspired people there continually lived the high ideal that in place of what brings strife and discord to human beings, that which can bring the good to earth must come. The good can be imagined through the symbol of the Cross entwined by the Roses.[5]

The Rosicrucian nature of the ideals of the Camphill founders certainly sounded through these words; and the refugees of the twentieth century had come to the place where the refugees of the Inquisition had already prepared the ground. It must have been like a waking call to Karl König to realise that these words were spoken by Rudolf Steiner on the day of König's fourteenth birthday, and that is the age at which – as Steiner told teachers – the real task of this incarnation begins to dawn and can be taken in hand by the young person. Reading this, König must have recognised his very own call from the spirit, and the call to those around him who were inspired by the same task.

A second birth moment

March 11 brings us to another 'birth moment' of what became the Camphill movement: the Anschluss of Austria by Nazi Germany happened on March 11, 1938. It was the moment that König decided to call the youth group together for a last time, to read a special content together, before each one should find their own way out of Central Europe. The content was the final lecture Rudolf Steiner gave at the Youth Course in Stuttgart in 1922. The intention was to meet again somewhere. In the essay 'Birth of a Movement' König wrote:

> We ... promised ourselves that we would faithfully carry our resolution to build a vehicle for Michael –

wherever that may be – which he could use to enter our civilisation. With this promise we took our leave of one another.

And in 'The Candle on the Hill':

We do not want to read anthroposophy; we want to live it. We decided to aim at starting a home for children with handicaps: the candle on the hill began to appear again before my inner vision.

And with this decision König began planning, even on his journey of exile through Italy, France and Switzerland. He did not want to be too far away from the geographic centre of Europe and applied to the governments of Cyprus and Ireland with a quite detailed plan. With the essay that König entitled 'Birth of a Movement' which he wrote close to the end of his life, it is of interest to see that, in looking back at the whole history of Camphill, he included two documents as appendices: the application to the Irish government and the opening address for Kirkton House.[6] The one is the first attempt to realise their vow to form a community somewhere, and the second is the founding moment in the North of Scotland.

A birth of Camphill was certainly only possible through this special intense community building back in Vienna, forming enthusiasm for spiritual content and initiating a kernel for the work which went through many trials, in turn inspired at least one further generation, and sowed seeds for the future.

A third element

A third element must be named in searching for the roots, or birth process of Camphill: that was König's quest for a new form of Christianity. The parable of the Good Samaritan had impressed him deeply as a child already and had given him a deep-seated motif for the challenges he increasingly experienced through his own powers of compassion and conscience. The socialist leanings of his youth led him eventually to study medicine and to link with anthroposophy. But it was a quest, not for Christian confession, but for a new form of Christianity, spiritually grounded and expressing itself in social reality – in *deeds*. On this quest, no doubt, meeting and working with Ita Wegman was an important factor; when writing the 'Requiem'[7] for her he puts her into close connection with Kaspar Hauser as a being working out of the forces of the Nathan Jesus and noted in his diary: 'She too was patient and calm, because she bore the new staff of Mercury, the sign of healing peace.' But probably the most significant encounter in this respect was with Mathilde Maasberg, who was then to become his wife.

After his first visit to her home in Silesia in May of 1928 he wrote in a letter about what he had experienced in the landscape formed and worked by generations of the Herrnhut Brethren: 'The innermost Christianity in your soul and the deep spirituality of the surrounding landscape' were a deep and – as he put it – redeeming experience for his soul. Indeed Tilla, as she was usually known, played a large part in the founding and forming of the Camphill movement. Without her religious devotion to the detail the ideals would probably not have 'grounded' so thoroughly. This element of practical self-development fired her own work but also became one of the guiding principles in the growing therapeutic and social Camphill environment. On their wedding anniversary, May 5, 1953, he wrote into his diary:

> This morning I thought back a lot to the time 24 years ago. The wedding and the first years of our marriage. Then I look into our wedding horoscope and am shaken to see that at the exact time of our wedding, the moon went through the 23rd degree of Virgo, the point at which many events related to the Grail occurred, also

INTRODUCTION

the laying of the Foundation Stone of the Goetheanum, but also the fire [of the Goetheanum], and the first Bible Evening in August of 1941. That then is the way it was destined. Apart from that, Jupiter is in a rising moon node and that is probably the indication for why the whole Community formed around Tilla and myself, [and] that this marriage was to become such a crystallisation point for the destinies of so many people and the focal point for social structures.

Tilla had grown up in and was influenced by the environment created by Count Zinzendorf and his followers. During his time in Silesia (1929–36) König made attempts to link the task of curative education to wider social needs and also to religious life. In the institution he co-founded in Pilgramshain there was a move to broaden the scope of the community, which included farming and medical work. König also travelled frequently to give courses (often with priests of the Christian Community) for social workers, nurses and teachers. This was through an initiative Ita Wegman had started in 1928, an Association for Social Support. Then in 1932 he founded his own Independent School for Social Work in Eisenach together with the priests Emil Bock and Friedrich Doldinger, but this institute soon had to be closed due to the political developments in Germany. After his flight to Scotland a new attempt could be made to build a holistic healing community against an ever darker backdrop of European and world developments. At the festive opening of Kirkton House, the 'forerunner' for what became Camphill, König said the following in his short address on Whitsunday of 1939:

> It is significant that we are here in Scotland, where the great Hibernian Mysteries were active which – although they were of pagan origin – received Christianity and contributed towards the Christianising of Great Britain.
> … If one travels through the countryside here, one can

15

have the impression that Christianity must be brought back and that is possible in a transformed way through Anthroposophy.

We must understand this rightly. It is not that we should see ourselves as the bearers of a mission, but that we should try to bring about a meeting between the English spirit and the spirit of Central Europe, a meeting between everything that has been dreamt and thought by the German spirit and that which the English spirit can accomplish by way of deeds. We should promise one another not to create an island of Central Europe here but to try as well as we can to act for the good of this land. We want to try to achieve this even in the knowledge that even if we fail, others will succeed. But let us try, and perhaps the spirit will allow us to make such a contribution.[8]

Inner and outer founding

Just one year later, on Whitsunday 1940, the menfolk were deported as 'enemy aliens' to the Isle of Man and the women had to keep the work going under difficult and uncertain circumstances, managing the move to Camphill House just a month later. It was the women who first moved into the old and needy Kirkton House, and now it was up to the women to make the decision for the future, and also to practically carry it out. At the same moment that this little group of hard-working pioneers outwardly 'founded' Camphill, the men were preparing an 'inner founding', working intensively on anthroposophic contents and gaining new friends who would follow them to their new home at Camphill House. König contributed strongly to these studies that took place in the seclusion of the internment camp. In particular he brought his seven years of work with the Calendar of the Soul to fruition by drawing meditative illustrations.[9]

INTRODUCTION

This work very much set a direction for the inner developments in Camphill and one can have the impression that nothing was done later without including the Calendar verses: König spoke about them at the festivals, in connection to embryology, to farming, to biography, and used them for the preparation of all therapeutic consultations about the children in Camphill. A book was compiled and hand-copied as guidance for the meditative work of his closest co-workers.[10] Another seven years later he formulated his experience in an address for Advent:

> The Soul Calendar can indeed be seen as a path of initiation that leads into the planetary sphere and thence to the sphere where the etheric Christ lives.

The other experience that König brought back from the Isle of Man was of a dream in which Count Zinzendorf appeared to him as his teacher proposing the institution of a regular celebration of the Gospels to imbue everyday life with forces of spiritual knowledge and love between brothers and sisters. This became the Bible Evening, a significant building stone and inner anchor-point for the growing Camphill movement. On August 30, 1953, Karl König gave a lecture about the history of the Bible Evening where he described:

> The Bible Evening is not a cult; it is just the opposite. The Bible Evening is the loving preparation of the human soul for the experience of the Cosmic Communion. This preparation is attempted through the Gospel and within a sphere wherein the light and the warmth of the living Christ can be experienced. Thus the Bible Evening prepares those who take part to become true human beings. When through the Gospel we learn to know ourselves, then we will gradually be able to celebrate the Cosmic Communion and fulfil the spiritual destiny of our age.

Again, a path of inner practice is meant, and again connected with a new form of Christianity.

Soon König connected the work of the pioneering group strongly with the Christian Community and already in 1945 there were ideas to found a real village settlement – what later became the 'Village' impulse in Botton – in the newly acquired estate of Newton Dee. König called it a therapeutic pastoral settlement. Peter Roth was sent to train as priest with the intention of being, together with the physician, Dr Gladstone, the centre of the community. Dr Gladstone did not actually join Camphill at all and Peter Roth only took up this role in Botton Village in 1956.

The priest from London, Alfred Heidenreich, had first met Karl König in 1928 at the World Conference of Spiritual Science in London and met him again in 1942 when Heidenreich was recuperating for a while in Aberdeen. He visited Camphill again in 1945 at the time when König formulated his First Memorandum, and in his surprise he commented that it was like the vows of a new form of an order. Indeed this question – whether the group should become an order or a community – was not new to the Königs as they had had to make that decision with their pioneering group in 1942. This group had asked Karl König to give rules of observance, but he was quite clear that a 'community' out of freedom and knowledge, and not out of rules, was the future path. That the description of the ideals written in the Memorandum echoed the mood of a brotherhood is, however, not to be denied. Later, in 1956, König wrote a short entry into his diary after a meeting, realising that they had after all taken the path of an order.

The words of the First Memorandum that lived on through many such developmental phases, are as follows:

> All who work in the Camphill Rudolf Steiner Schools
> in such a way that they do not claim any payment in the
> usual sense, but:

INTRODUCTION

    Who do their work
out of love for the children,
the sick,
the suffering;
out of love for the soil,
the gardens and fields, the woods
and everything which is
in the realm of the Community –
Who wish to do the work of their hands
out of devotion to Christ-Being
who has reappeared
in the ether sphere of the earth –
all who are thus willing
to act for the true progress of mankind
and who are consequently prepared
to sacrifice their self-willing
to the Spirit-willing;
Who will fashion their lives
according to the striving
towards the Spirit of our age
as it has been revealed
through Rudolf Steiner,
and as it is manifest
in the Sacraments
of the Christian Community
as well as in the Cosmic Communion
of the single human soul
that wrestles for its development;
    all these who are willing to work out of this
striving may call themselves members of the Camphill
Community.

The famous photographer Edith Tudor Hart, who was certainly more connected to socialism than to any form of organised religion, recognised clearly this elementary Christian striving when she compiled an article together with Fyfe Robertson for the *Picture Post* in April 1949, which was entitled 'A School where Love is a Cure,' and states:

> Individual treatment is the chief secret of Camphill's success. The basic treatment for all is good, naturally-grown, balanced food; intelligent medical care; a serene and regular life, and, above all, the affection which these children need, and which can sometimes make them flower wonderfully.
>
> Dr König is a deeply religious man, and his staff, too, approach their work almost in the spirit of a religious order … Unlike too many nominal Christians, they look upon a human being not as a body 'with a soul', but as a soul with a body. Here is of course a significant difference.

A page from the Picture Post, April 1949

INTRODUCTION

Diversity

Studying Karl König's various descriptions of the task and intentions of Camphill one can certainly say, yes, it is much wider than simply institutions for people with special needs, but at the same time the care of such children and adults was and remains central. It is important to keep this apparent paradox in mind. Probably the best indication of how this belongs together is to be found in the essay 'The Purpose and Value of Curative-Educational Work,' written towards the end of his life, in 1965. Here König describes the 'general' purpose of curative education, but obviously it is *his* view and the direction chosen for the curative movement *he* founded. Towards the end of the essay he sums up:

> We only need to define the concept of curative education widely enough to see its true purpose ... Its intention is to become a global task to help counteract the 'threat to the individual person' which has arisen everywhere. The 'curative educational attitude' needs to express itself in any social work, in pastoral care, in the care for the elderly, in the rehabilitation of mentally ill and physically handicapped people, in the guidance of orphans and refugees, of suicidal and desperate individuals, in the international Peace Corps and similar ambitions.[11]

It is a wide purpose that he sees here and underlines that by studying the parallel development of curative education and the decline of social coherence in society. Already in his 'Report to the Movement' after the Camphill Movement Council had met on January 28, 1960, he said:

> Dear friends,
> Last year, at the end of my Annual Report I asked the question: is the Movement identical with curative

education only? And then we had tentatively to say: it is not. And we said: wherever the image of man (some of you will remember it) is distorted and humiliated, the Movement is going to have its place. And this is another important step. Because we now have to work for curative education – and this will continue; and perhaps with this all our new settlements may start. But we have now also the branch of the villages: and, dear friends, it will not always be a village for young men and women with handicaps – it may be, in all what is going to come, that it will be a village for stranded people, a village in Africa ... [or] a village in Malaya, a village here and there: because the economic life of the world is going to break down and village seeds will have to be sown here and there and in many other places. Therefore I foresee this branch as a very important one – not confined at all to Botton and the Grange, but giving many more possibilities if we are permitted and allowed to start them.

König saw the importance of community building out of anthroposophy for the future development of society altogether, and in this those with special needs can be our teachers and leading images. Community is crucial that the individual is able to develop at all; this is the theme he particularly demonstrates in lectures towards the end of his life, collected in the volume that bears his words as title, *Becoming Human: a Social Task*. And he intended Camphill to play a role in this – being a forerunner for future needs in social development. John the Baptist was called the forerunner, and from the internment camp in 1940 König had designated St John as an inspiring image for the pioneer group – 'but we are only forerunners of the forerunners' he often told his friends. This connection to John played an important part in the following decades.[12]

In a letter to Community members in 1948 König pointed to the task of community building but – in keeping with his

INTRODUCTION

First Memorandum – a community which is open for all but to which not everyone needs to belong as Community *member,* it is a community out of anthroposophy for our times and not for a select group, brotherhood or sect. This letter became then what is known as the Second Memorandum:

> The institutions in Camphill have come about through the fact that anthroposophy as the true spiritual impulse of our age has lightened up in the souls of the members or through the fact that the Community itself has been experienced by newcomers as an ideal to which they desire to devote themselves. Thus out of spiritual impulses which led to life-decisions, the working structure of the Community arose. But now people have entered these institutions who, for instance, do not meet the Community with sufficient understanding; or also people who gladly accept the forms of life of the Community but are not sufficiently close to anthroposophy because their souls are not so constituted that they are able to accept it ... Also the children and young people live in this atmosphere but do not belong to the Community.* With this the Community is given a special task, the fulfilment of which requires much tact and insight, for the institutions must be there for all people, but not the Community. The Community must maintain a wakeful eye for the institutions it brings about and it must serve those people who wish to live in its atmosphere.

During the Second World War Camphill had already developed to be something of a holistic community, where research was done, crafts and trades were beginning to be incorporated, and many arts were included, in shaping the environment to become

---

* Adults with special needs were not yet being looked after in Camphill – only children and youngsters.

part of the healing impulse, or directly as artistic therapies. Music, painting, sculpture, architecture, design, speech and eurythmy were practised and presented, colour therapy and colour light therapy were being developed and König was connected to the budding movement of music therapy; very diverse themes and vocations were being addressed with conferences and workshops. A very full guest book of the 1940s bears witness to the many visitors from all over Europe and from further afield – astonishing for the decade of the Second World War. In 1950, as the Camphill movement really began to expand to the South of England, Karl König stated a far-sighted aim in a letter to Carlo Pietzner, one of the Viennese youth group who was to pioneer the Camphill movement in its westward growth – first to Northern Ireland in 1953 and then in 1960 to the United States. As Pietzner was looking for suitable houses in England König wrote:

> Curative education alone is not our sole purpose, but rather with and through those with special needs to create cultural islands.[13]

And in 1956, with his opening address for the first village community in Botton, North Yorkshire, König not only accentuates the social, cultural task for society, but also speaks in a way – even if the words carry a colouring of the time – that seems to already hint at the task of equality and inclusion. The ideals of the Camphill Villages that König spoke about again and again from various angles amount to a form of 'inversed inclusion' – creating a healing and future-bearing social environment as can help those with special needs to find their path in life and to themselves, which in turn will prove to be a healing and invigorating setting for any human being. This can work 'outwards' into society, but also invite many into life-sharing and reciprocally enhancing intentional communities. Indeed this process has been experienced by many individuals in

INTRODUCTION

a significant and life changing way. König ends his talk by naming three far-reaching yet tangible tasks of the village:

The Camphill village could be a vital experiment for future social needs. Men and women whose intelligence is, according to test standards, supposed to be inferior, will live and work with others of 'normal' intelligence, but will not regard this as a barrier between them, for it is an illusory barrier. Every human being is endowed with the same intelligence; it is the talent given to each of us when we are born. The spark can he clouded or paralysed, existentially frustrated, imprisoned in a damaged body, yet it is just here where all human beings are *equal*. To acknowledge this will help the 'normal' to overcome their pride, for it is pride which divides humankind into the clever and the stupid, the primitive and the advanced, the higher and the lower of their kind.

A second task is to experience that the human origin does not lie in the natural alone, but that it lies equally in the transcendent. This needs daily practice in which we shall continuously have to contend with our own weaknesses and unbelief. We shall be confronted with daily disappointment and despair. Others will not live up to our expectations and we ourselves shall soon lose heart and faith. We shall then have to be mindful of the divine seed in every human being, a seed powerful enough to overcome all difficulties and trials – if not today, then tomorrow; if not tomorrow, then later, ultimately. Here, there is a solemn *fraternity* among all people. We are brothers and sisters because we originate in the Divine and the Divine is at the same time our human potential and the incentive in our human development.

Finally, we must learn that all our work and efforts are in vain if not sustained by a sense of divine meaning. Common work, common worship, common deed and common joy, common sorrow, and commonly experienced grace, gradually create the certainty of a Divine Presence, which is a community experience of the rarest wonder.

When we succeed in kindling our enthusiasm and our love for the work we do every day, whether it is baking bread, making shoes, milking cows, we shall gain *freedom*, for true freedom can only be experienced when we devote our labours in love to a Higher Meaning.

Thus in a community can *three great ideals* of modern mankind be realised – Liberty, Equality and Fraternity – ideals that were trampled into dust and blood in the French Revolution, and which are waiting to be raised anew.

These three great ideals, when brought forward into vital social living, will counteract and heal the effects of the three great errors of today's society. The Camphill Village is an active endeavour to contribute to this task. The outcasts of today are the forerunners of the future![14]

With the 'return' to Central Europe, which was of such great importance to König, he was able to express some of his ideals for Camphill in a special way. In 1958 the first Camphill School could open in Brachenreuthe, Lake Constance and could be extended through the opening of a second school community in Föhrenbühl. There, at the official opening in May 1964 he said:

> It is now thirty-six years that I began to work for children with handicaps. To begin I was extremely stupid. Not that I am much more clever now, but I have gained experience and begin to recognise what it is that we speak of in curative education. There is one fundamental recognition I realise ever more, the older I grow: a children's home is a beautiful thing a residential school is a good arrangement, an institution for remedial education

is a very effective instrument for helping these children ... All this is right. But as long as it is only a children's home, or only residential school, or boarding school, it is not yet what these children and adolescents who are given in our care really need. A bunch of flowers is beautiful, a twig full of blossoms is wonderful, but the bush is missing, the roots are missing, the ground is missing out of which all this grows. It remains artificial. It can only become complete, natural and real, when such a home, school or institution does not exist for itself alone, but becomes a community of life, embedded in a community of life ...

Man is a social being and without this, he is only half a human being. A home is beautiful, but it is only right if it is a part of a social community of work and life. This, I believe, to be the case in all our homes, schools and institutions. What I imagine of this growing child, Föhrenbühl, is a place where children will be guided, educated, healed, where adolescents will be introduced to work on the land, in the gardens, that we should build a home for old people, where parents of our co-workers can live, that we establish a small farm and that all the people who will live here in the manifoldness of their work and tasks, will form a social living community. Then there would be the certainty that those children who have to be taken out of their families would be permitted to enter a different, though equally valuable social living community. Only where human beings settle down together, work together and for one another, strive together, where big and small, important and unimportant, clever and less clever, in mutual respect for the dignity of each individual, meet one another and build up a new community – not out of bonds of blood, but out of spirit bonds – there arises the framework in which children, young people, adults, who have not received what has been given to others, can live in such a way that their innermost being and spiritual existence can be expressed and find its rightful place. Therefore, I hope that such a living and working community will be built up here in Föhrenbühl.

König continues then to express how this work becomes possible through the ideals given by Rudolf Steiner, and ends thus:

> At Michaelmas, when we opened this house quite unofficially first of all, we called it 'The house of good fruits.'
> Out of the fundamental social law alone, these fruits can ripen:
> 'In a community of human beings working together, the well-being of the community will be the greater, the less the individual claims for himself the proceeds of the work he has himself done; that is, the more of these proceeds he makes over to his fellow workers, and the more his own requirements are satisfied not out of his own work done, but out of work done by the others.'
> Should we be able to put this into practice, even if only to a small extent, there will be sown into the earth of mankind a good seed. This answers the needs of our time, in which so much destruction has to be carried as destiny.

And sixteen months later, on his own last birthday here on earth, he was able to give a moving address for the opening of the first village community in Germany, at Lehenhof, not far from the schools. One senses that it was a very special moment for König:

> In these so-called retarded children and adults there lives and becomes outwardly apparent, for the most part, far

more humanity than comes to manifestation in those of us who are busy and active. And it is by no means the case that these children and adults, who are constantly on the increase in the modern world, live among us as a burden. In times to come people will look back on our century and say: we were the people who gradually had to learn that the outsiders are the ones who have begun to lead us back to the path of honesty ... and when such villages arise they exemplify this reawakened humanity. Dear friends, this is the only thing that we want.[15]

This high aim König states as 'the only thing we want'! One has the impression that this work in such village settlements that later became known as social therapy was intended to be much more than holistic therapy or rehabilitation for people with learning difficulties and other special needs, but that this 'social experiment', as König called it at the end of his course for village co-workers,[16] as therapeutic measure, as a healing deed towards society as a whole.

At the founding of the first village community in Botton in 1955 König points to the fact that this impulse had had to wait for ten years (from the first intentions for Newton Dee in 1945) and in his address for the official opening, in May 1956, he quotes the fundamental significance of community with the words of T.S. Eliot:

What life have you if you have not life together?
There is no life that is not in community,
And no community not lived in praise of God.[17]

It is moving to read the entry Karl König made in his diary during the year of his serious illness, after not being able to actively take part in life for months and with the prognosis that his life was ending soon, we read the words written on his birthday, September 25, 1955:

I feel that Camphill has become a spiritual space in which many searching souls are able to find their home. That is a wonderful gift.

Becoming a movement

When did Camphill become a movement? In her *History of the Camphill Community Since 1954*, Anke Weihs stated:

> In connection with the inception of *The Cresset* as the Journal of Camphill in 1954, the term 'Camphill Movement' came into usage to signify not only the waxing conglomerate of Camphill places in Britain, including the first Village Community at Botton and then places overseas, but also a peculiar qualitative force of social compassion for which Kaspar Hauser and the challenges arising from his existence were a symbol.

This mention of Kaspar Hauser in immediate connection to the birth and purpose of the Camphill movement is certainly notable. In the same community meeting, Michaelmas 1945, where König presented his colleagues with the First Memorandum, Alix Roth made the following notes of what he said in connection to the document:

> Today in our talk with Dr Gladstone I could experience the opposing [*sic*] forces, which work – fight – against the Community. Never before in such a clarity, did they stand before me. But never before had they melted away like this, like snow in the sun. What are the names of the forces – powers – which stand against our innermost task? For the first time I could call these names: Meyer, Stanhope, Hickel. All those who stood up against Kaspar Hauser. The image of man is attacked. But you see, K.H. was murdered

by Lord Stanhope, therefore we are in Britain, and we have to solve the destiny of all who stood up against K.H. Only through continuous service and sacrifice can we do that, because we have to carry the image of man so strongly in our existence, that they become aware of having it also within themselves. Kaspar Hauser died and 6 times 18 years and 7 months later, we have the Memorandum in our hands – hearts. Through this it might be possible that the image of man will shine into the realm of the soul – help to enlighten the spirit. We will learn to form the heart when we learn to understand the task of K.H. This heart will never fail, if we do it in devotion.[18]

Directly after he war had ended a stream of new co-workers from Germany and other European countries began to come to the North of Scotland where the ground had been prepared. Soon the possibility arose for extending the work southwards and westwards, and particularly back to the European mainland. In 1950 there were 250 children and young adults in the five centres around Aberdeen with over 100 coworkers.

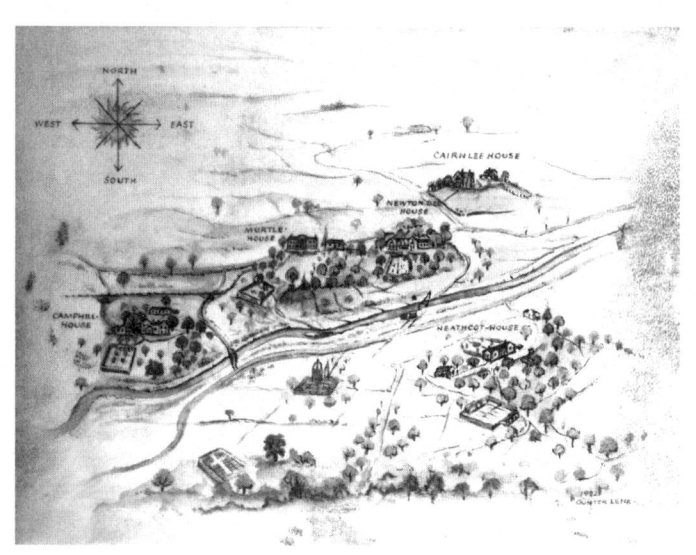

Map of Camphill Schools, drawn 1952 by Günther Lehr

By 1960 Newton Dee had become a village community; two school communities existed in southern England (Ringwood and Thornbury) and a village community was at the Grange, near Bristol; in the North of England Botton Village was well established and had started a Waldorf School; Glencraig School with training centre was in Northern Ireland. Beginnings had been made in South Africa with Dawn Farm. In the United States the start of a school was imminent with Downingtown School in Pennsylvania, and talks had begun for the start of a village in New York State. In Central Europe Brachenreuthe school and farm had begun as well as Huize Christophorus in Holland, and the search for a suitable setting for a village community was underway. Initiatives in Switzerland and Norway had not yet come to fruition.

The official opening of Glencraig, Northern Ireland in 1954

INTRODUCTION

Karl König in South Africa, 1957

Karl König giving a seminar in Donegal Springs, Pennsylvania, 1962

Karl König at the opening of the Lehenhof Village, with Ruth Lohmann, founder of the German Camphill Friends Association, and Georg von Arnim, September 25, 1965

In various meetings of the Camphill Movement Council König expressed his concerns that the inner impulse of the Camphill Community may not be strong enough to carry and sustain the rapid expansion and necessary diversity of the Camphill movement. But his colleagues were often surprised at his openness for change and new aspects. In 1960 such a passage is to be found in his report of the Council meeting:

> A year ago, dear friends, everyone of us would have been at a certain loss to explain squarely and clearly what the movement is. We would have said we know what the movement is, we experience the movement; we might have said: the movement is an impulse, it is initiative, it is something to which several people, centres, schools belong: but there was no self-recognition that we would visualise the movement in an appropriate way. This has started to come about. And it has found its first expression in the article which I could write in the Christmas issue of the *Cresset;* this article is called 'Meditations on the Camphill Movement.'[19] During the last year a certain unifying process has set in within the movement and this unifying process has given rise it a certain amount of self-recognition. We know that above the movement there shone the three stars of Comenius, of Zinzendorf and of Owen, and that another rejuvenation through spiritual science of Rudolf Steiner permeates our existence within the Movement. We have come thus far.

What is the connection of Camphill itself and the Camphill movement? The movement has accepted what Camphill has given to it. And the question is, is this process going on? Is it to go on, and if it is to go on, how will it go on? It is perhaps necessary that Camphill has to sacrifice itself in order that the movement may grow? Or will that the movement rather work back on to Camphill

INTRODUCTION

*The Movement Council inspects the building site
for Camphill Hall in Murtle estate in 1961*

in order to rejuvenate it? I would not venture to give an answer, but I would beg you, dear friends, to keep this question in mind. To move it in your hearts. Because it is a very important question. And again only life will teach us to give the right answer: intellectually you cannot solve it, by discussing you cannot solve it, none of us could solve it. We can only listen to the signs and watch the symptoms. A new group, from a younger generation, has taken over Camphill just over a year ago. Through this decision it was possible to bring about what I could describe to you tonight as the life and the being of the movement. But now we have to be very watchful, to see what the mother, Camphill, is expecting from the movement – what the child needs from the mother: and how these two entities are going to work together.

And in 1964 we find the following passage, showing how König wanted to do justice to the needs of the growing movement:

35

So we decided in the last Movement Council Meeting, which in fact *was* the *last* Movement Council Meeting, to divide, to differentiate the movement and proposed that from now on there should be six regions. Each one of these six regions should create its own movement council, thus six plus one would be seven movement councils ... one in the United States under the chairmanship of Carlo [Pietzner]; the second one in South Africa under the chairmanship of Dr [Hans Müller-] Wiedemann; the third one in Central Europe, of which I would take over the chairmanship; the fourth one the Schools in England and Scotland under the chairmanship of Thomas [Weihs]; the fifth the Villages in Scotland and England under the chairmanship of Peter [Roth]; and the sixth the Schools and Village Centre in Northern Ireland, together with Holland and with the coming work in Scandinavia under the chairmanship of Hans-Heinrich [Engel]. I beg you earnestly to see this, dear friends, to see this new step, this new chapter, as opening up the book of the history of the movement. We are embarking on a very new venture.

This 'new venture' meant further diversification according to local circumstances and a process of metamorphosis of the structure of the regions and their interrelationship, the new Camphill Hall in Murtle being a focal point for at least two decades, and with the group named evolving as the Camphill Movement Group, which still exists today.

The more detailed history of the Camphill movement and the challenges and questions involved in today's situation can not be the task of this publication. Suffice it to say that in 2010 *Portrait of Camphill* (edited by Jan Bang) was published to give a picture of the history and the developments in the various regions. Research and detailed publications about current questions is ongoing.[20]

INTRODUCTION

What does Camphill stand for?

Recalling König's reference to the French Revolution quoted above, one could almost sum up the task he saw through curative work for society of the future by using the title of a book by Kurt Becker aimed at creating contemporary understanding for anthroposophy in general, 'Revolution from Within'.

The danger is not to be denied today that the significance of people with special needs for society may be lost through inclusion into a society which is not ready and not sufficiently equipped for that 'specialness' and which is not structured nor fired by the quest for the spiritual nature and task of the individual on his and her path to becoming truly human.

Indeed this high aim of the Camphill community has to do with the individuality of Kaspar Hauser as König describes him in his essay and more poetically in his *Christmas Story*.[21] From notes Karl König made and from the report published later in a German medical journal,[22] we know that he spoke in an enthusing way about this significance at the opening lecture of an international curative conference in Zeist, Holland in 1948. He spoke of an 'inner stream running through Central European history,' mentioning Novalis, Goethe and Beethoven, and then stating that this stream was forced into obscurity in the nineteenth century, leaving mankind with the 'sphinx-riddle' – what is the human being – and with a battle between Goetheanism and Darwinism. Into this situation Kaspar Hauser is placed as the child of Europe, the image of the human being. He then ended his lecture with a plea to realise that curative education is a necessity of our times. His notes suggest that he spoke similarly in Bristol on August 1, 1943, in the middle of the Second World War. It was just a few months after the death of Ita Wegman, for whom he had written the 'Requiem,' mainly about Kaspar Hauser.[23] In his notes for Bristol, where he spoke to parents about curative education, we read:

These children are not a danger, they are a remedy to mankind. Because in these children the cosmic being of man is revealed ... Build a society where everybody can live. Kaspar Hauser, the child of Europe.

Kaspar Hauser becomes an image for the person with special needs. Particularly after 1953, when König was able to lecture in Germany and began to look for a starting point for Camphill there, we find in notes or even in lecture titles the name of Kaspar Hauser and the term 'the children of Europe'.

Finally, in asking what the central aim of Camphill actually is, we can look to the year in which König began to spend more and more time in Central Europe, moving there in 1964. In his report from the Movement Council, on February 1, 1963, he asked precisely this question, calling it the *Ur-Impuls,* the archetypal endeavour, of Camphill. With this he then referred back to his 'Candle on the Hill' experience in 1927, linking on to the three 'Stars' and Rudolf Steiner as a fourth leading individuality (these three and the fourth will be discussed in the introduction to the 3 essays later in the book):

> But in order to find the new image for Thornbury, Sheiling, and so on, I feel, dear friends, it is necessary that we turn to the *Ur-Impuls* of Camphill. And the Movement Council has decided that we should hold a conference on remedial education after the start of the holidays in July, here in the [newly-built Camphill] Hall [in Murtle, Aberdeen]. It should be a conference for the movement and some of the friends of the movement. It should concern itself with the *Ur-Impuls* of Camphill. But I would suggest, dear friends that already now in the various places ... here and on the continent, and in South Africa and in the United States, we should prepare ourselves for the rediscovery of the *Ur-Impuls* of Camphill: to reawaken in the child with special needs

INTRODUCTION

the image of man. Not to look for something which appears to be majestic or grandiose – but to know that to help one or two or three children to become what they are: that is our task. Through many demands, through many necessary specialisations, we time and again forget this *Ur-Impuls*, and then it is, dear friends, as if we would lose the ring of our allegiance to Camphill, to the spirit of Camphill, to the image of Kaspar Hauser. The Hall is built and the Hall should serve to re-kindle this *Ur-Impuls*.

And if you would now like to draw a last conclusion, in order to look into the next years to come, I would have to say: let us try to keep the three stars of the movement alight and alive. From the Hall, this universal knowledge should go out for which Comenius was fighting. Regaining the *Ur-Impuls* will kindle all that which Zinzendorf was aiming for when he began to found his religious communities. And the Village impulse itself is no doubt the beginning of a fulfilment for which Robert Owen has striven throughout his life. We should not forget the presence of these three individualities. But we should by no means forget, dear friends, what some of us have experienced ever more strongly in the course of the last few months; and this is the presence of Rudolf Steiner. I think I know that he has shown a remarkable interest, active interest, extended in love for what we are trying to do. Perhaps it is on account of the Hall that he is now for us more consciously helping our efforts. That this may go on, ever stronger and stronger – so that we in the end are a real tool in his hand and a mouthpiece for his message – this I think would be wonderful.

To end on a personal note, I remember taking part in a youth gathering leading up to an international conference in 1980 that became significant for many young people. We had the good fortune to have Anke Weihs as guest and heard from her, how Camphill should not become a 'brand name' but that ever more people – especially young people – learn to understand the roots and ideals of Camphill in such a way that they become motifs of our heart which can become fruitful in whatever the situation at hand happens to be.

Much later I realised how she was linking on for us to the youth group in Vienna of 1938, reading about the task of the Archangel Michael and pledging to work for this in the future. All would have been well and we could have finished the meeting that had anyway been much longer than planned, but then one of the newer members of the group interjected innocently, 'But what *is* Camphill?' Some of us feared more hours of sitting in order to answer that fundamental question which we anyway found totally misplaced. Anke Weihs, however, calmly and as if she were hoping for just this question, simply said: 'Camphill is to will the future.' The evening ended in rich silence and most of us took at least this into our hearts.

Richard Steel
Berlin, New Year 2017/18

Outcasts in Scotland: Pioneers in an Old Manse

During the years of 1936 and 1937, a few young men and women gathered around a country doctor who had come to Vienna, the town of his birth, to build up a medical practice in one of the suburbs of that city. The doctor and his wife had been forced to leave Germany where he had worked for some time by the conditions Nazism imposed.

Under this doctor's guidance, the group of young people began to study anthroposophy and many an evening was spent in reading, studying and discussing Rudolf Steiner's work. The group consisted of young teachers, medical students and a few artists. All of them had one thing in mind and that was not only to understand anthroposophy and to listen to the teachings of Rudolf Steiner, but to basically change their attitude to life. They felt more or less clearly that Nazism was a sign that destructive forces in the world were coming to a peak and that something would have to be done to counteract this evil force. But they knew that counter-action by means of force or mass movement would not be effective. They felt rather that a new understanding of the human being and all nature, and a devotional attitude to life in all its manifestations through living Christianity would be the necessary counterbalance to Nazism. Through Rudolf Steiner's teaching, they learned that thoughts and ideals alone would change nothing, but a change of attitude to life could do very much. They decided to start a community outside a town, working the soil, educating children and educating themselves through daily work, daily study and daily devotion.

Then Nazism also flooded Austria and these young people had to leave the country with the hope of finding one another again in some other place still free from oppression and racialism which would be helpful in allowing people to live their lives as they think best. Each of these young men and women went through many adventures and setbacks. They had fled to Italy, Switzerland, France, Yugoslavia, Czechoslovakia, Holland and Britain. They often had no contact with one another and experienced much hardship and loneliness, until finally they all came to Britain where they decided to ask the authorities to agree to support their ideas of starting a community.

Through chance and destiny, some helpful members of the Church of Scotland became interested and other friends in the north-east of Scotland offered a house on their own estate to the little group of refugees.

This house was an abandoned manse standing on a hill and overlooking a wide valley north of Aberdeen. It was the first actual roof over the heads of this small group. The estate owners provided them with potatoes, milk and oatmeal. The doctor had

Kirkton House from above

Part of Douglas on the Isle of Man that became an internment camp

been able to bring his furniture over from Austria and after a few weeks, the manse was ready for occupation. The garden was dug, the walls painted, the debris and dust cleared from the outhouses, and after two months, the first handicapped children arrived and the fees paid for them privately made it possible to begin to live a regular life. The good and strong ideals and the will to stick to them on the part of these few people overcame all difficult circumstances; and this was encouraging and grand to see.

May 12, 1940, was a fateful day for the community, because on this Whitsunday, all the men were interned and sent to the Isle of Man. The women were left alone and to begin with they were uncertain as to whether to carry on what was begun or wait until the men returned. But they decided to carry on, and not only that; they decided to extend the work.

Just before the internment of the men took place, the community had many inquiries for places for children. The manse was too small to envisage taking any more children and so the community tried to find a better and a bigger place. Owing to the unforgettable kindness of a friend and father of one of the boys who was due to join us, Camphill estate was purchased

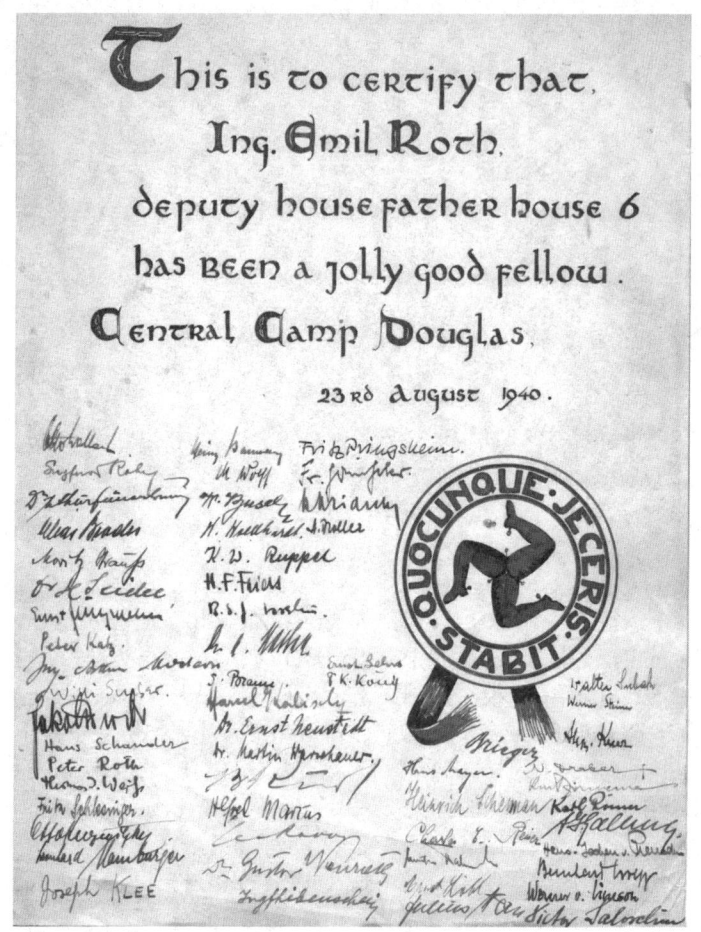

> **This is to certify that,**
> **Ing. Emil Roth,**
> **deputy house father house 6**
> **has been a jolly good fellow.**
> **Central Camp Douglas,**
>
> 23rd August 1940.

'Certificate' for Emil Roth from his house mates at dismissal with signatures of Hans Schauder, Peter Roth, Thomas Weihs, Willi Sucher, Ernst Lehrs, Karl König

and ready to receive us. Everything for the move to Camphill had been prepared and the date fixed when the men were interned and the move seemed for a moment impossible. But the women were full of confidence and strength and faith. They moved to the new place on June 1, 1940, furnished the house, worked the gardens and fields, took care of the children and struggled through the early months until in October the first two men came back from internment camp, finding everything in the best of order.

From now on, the work gradually enlarged. The community now has a big house, a cottage and lodge and 22 acres of ground. Throughout the winter, we had our own potatoes and a lot of fruit and vegetables. We have ten children and some more to come. Most of the men have returned from internment and the work is running according to our aims. We shall soon have some goats and pigs and already have hens. We hope to acquire a cow in the near future. So again, faith and confidence guided the community through hard and bitter times to a better standard.

View from Camphill House over the gardens and the River Dee (from König's photo album, with his title 'What will the future be?') It is their first photograph of Camphill, before the move in 1940.

Our future aims

What we have established up till now has been described. But what are our further aims? The true aims are to become a real community connected with the work on the land and in the house, connected with our own children and those who have been given into our care. Handicapped children are mostly outcasts of human society. They are children who are unable to speak or unable to work. Children who are unable to find a place in their own homes, who cannot find schools and training. We want to try to share our work with them, to show them how to hold a spade and to dig, how to make a compost heap and how to plant vegetables. But we also want to show them how to learn about and understand the world, to teach them to appreciate the beauty of the world and the kindness of people. We want to try to teach them to understand numbers, music, to help them to read and write, to teach them to paint and model and carve. We shall have common meals, common joys and common sorrows. We shall have the Sunday Services with our children. And our children will begin to establish themselves in the community and find their own identities, because their environment is one of love and understanding.

We hope to receive more and more handicapped children. We hope in time to build a few more small houses for them and to establish a tiny village in which there is a community of outcasts who are not outcasts but active citizens who will make their own contribution, and who have faith in what is spiritual and love for one another.

These are our aims.

But there may be a question in the mind of the reader: why do we want to make all this effort on behalf of handicapped children? Is it worthwhile, when there are perhaps more important tasks in these troubled times?

The Candle on the Hill

The following is an attempt to describe the early history of Camphill. It is naturally bound to be subjective in its outlook as it is to a certain extent my own story. To a great degree, my life is identical with Camphill – with its foundation as well as with its later development. I shall, however, try to be as objective as possible and simply describe without giving too many interpretations.

Camphill was not created within a few weeks. It took many years before the single threads of destiny began to find one another and weave a pattern on the loom of life. Nor was Camphill the result of external circumstances although they played a certain part and modelled special features into the structure of its existence. It was not altogether necessary that Camphill should have started in Scotland; I could imagine that another place somewhere in the realm of the English-speaking world would have been equally well-suited. But Camphill was certainly meant to become part of the western world and not of the eastern. Its aims are occidental and not oriental. Yet it does not consider itself to be of western origin. Its roots are in Central Europe and it acts as an ambassador of mid-European culture. How far we have succeeded in this task is not for us to judge. Camphill, now being twenty-one years old, is coming of age; it begins to consider its own background and to understand its foundations.

Work with Ita Wegman

When I ask myself where to look for the first dim beginnings of the story of Camphill, I see myself standing on the platform of one of the railway stations in Vienna, waiting for a train. It was a late evening in the early autumn of 1927. Several months previously, I had taken my medical degree at the University of Vienna and was now working in one of the big hospitals for sick children, trying to gain as much experience as possible so that I would soon be able to set up my own medical practice.

I stood there on the platform, reserved and uncomfortable, because with a few friends, I had been invited to welcome Dr Ita Wegman who was coming to Vienna. She was to attend the funeral of Rudolf Steiner's only sister who had died two days before. Along with a few others, I was asked to greet Dr Wegman. I had never met her before and constantly asked myself why it was necessary for me to wait for somebody I did not know. I was at the time rather young and shy and did not really like to be among many people.

At last the train pulled into the station and Dr Wegman alighted, accompanied by several friends. She greeted the welcoming part. I was introduced to her, we shook hand and all was over. I left the station very quickly and went home, not knowing what it was all about. A few days later I was invited to attend a party at the house of a wealthy timber merchant where I was to meet Dr Wegman again as she had expressed the wish to have a word with me. I went to the party and was later ushered into a room where I found myself face to face with her. She was at the time leader of the Medical Faculty of the School of Spiritual Science at Dornach. During the last three years of Rudolf Steiner's life, she was his closest pupil and collaborator and nursed him during his severe illness in 1924/25. She was also the head of the Medical-Therapeutical Institute [now the Ita Wegman Clinic] in Arlesheim near Basle, close to Dornach.

I felt quite at ease when I sat opposite her and she asked me a few questions about my life and work and then suggested that I join her clinic in Arlesheim. I was astonished at this offer, but happy at the prospect of being introduced so closely to the work of anthroposophical therapeutics. So I asked her when she would expect me to go, thinking that it might be some time ahead after I had concluded my clinical year in Vienna. Dr Wegman looked at me with a gracious smile and suggested that I go to Arlesheim in about a couple of weeks. I got a slight shock and said that this was out of the question. But she would not give in and so we agreed that I would be in Arlesheim at the beginning of November. I then left her, inspired by her great personality which I had immediately recognised.

On November 7, 1927 I arrived in Arlesheim.[1] It took me a number of days before I was able to find my way through the maze of people and activities going on around me. Everything was new, and to begin with I was unable to discover any order or plan in the daily routine of that place. There were doctors and students, patients and visitors, nurses and chemists and everyone went his way and was not in the least interested in helping me. *Frau Doktor* was away in Holland and nobody expected my arrival. I did not feel that I was welcomed at all. After these first, rather excruciating days, Dr Wegman returned and took the reins again into her own hands.

I was assigned work in the research laboratory as well as in the Sonnenhof. The latter was a home for children with handicaps, and when I visited it, I met this type of child for the first time in my life. I still remember the immediate response I felt towards these human beings. A great well of love and compassion I had never experienced before surged forth. I see myself sitting down on the floor and playing with some of the children as soon as I saw them.

From now on I went to the Sonnenhof daily. I attended the children medically under Dr Wegman's guidance; I tried to understand their handicaps and shortcomings. My first love for

Karl König with nurses at the clinic in Arlesheim in 1929 for whom he was giving a course

them did not vanish or diminish, and I may say that they, too, liked me very much. They responded to me immediately and quickly became my friends.

On the first Advent Sunday, I had the unique experience of the Advent garden festival. Never before had I ever heard anything about Advent; at that time, it was an unknown festival in Austria. But now I saw myself sitting in a circle with my children and their helpers. In the centre of the room there was a little mound built up of earth and covered with moss and on top of it stood a large burning candle. Around the mound, a spiral of moss had been laid out, reaching far into the room; it almost touched the circle of children. Each child, holding in its hand an apple into which a small candle was fixed, had to walk along the spiral to light its own candle at the central candle on the hill. The people sitting round sang Christmas carols and the whole mood was one of reverent joy and happiness. The faces of the children were radiant as each one tried very hard to perform the task of walking and reaching out their little hand to light their own candle at the candle on the hill.

My own heart flowed over with compassion. I saw these severely handicapped beings who appeared so happy and bright. I suddenly and profoundly experienced that the spark of the living spirit was present in each one of them in spite of their disabilities.

And in this hour, the decision was taken that I would dedicate my life to the care and education of these children. It was a promise I gave myself: to build a hill upon which a big candle was to burn so that many children, infirm and with handicaps, would be able to find their way to this beacon of hope and to light their own candles so that each single flame would be able to radiate and shine forth.

At this moment I did not know that the hill would in time bear the name Camp-hill. An ideal started to grow in my mind and heart.

Advent garden

Finding a task

Four weeks later I gave my first lecture at the Goetheanum. It was during the annual Christmas Conference and I stood in the same place and put my hand on the same pulpit whence a few years before Rudolf Steiner had so often spoken. I was still a very young man and quite aware of the honour and the responsibility I bore at that moment.

I spoke to the vast audience of several hundred people about the early development of the human embryo and of how the then newly discovered facts were a distinct proof of the descriptions Rudolf Steiner had given of the evolution of man and earth. I started and closed the lecture with the image of Raphael's *Sistine Madonna*.

The impression my deliberations made was rather far-reaching. I was at once asked to continue to lecture at the Goetheanum and if possible, to remain there as a teacher. I was very astonished at this offer as I had not realised that my task was such an outstanding success. In the course of the following days, I received a number of invitations to speak in various towns in Germany. I was very happy with these new opportunities and discussing everything with Dr Wegman, I had her blessing to go on a lecture-tour.

But before telling about this journey which was to become another crucial event in the preparation for Camphill, I must mention something else. It is a more personal matter, yet one which fundamentally belongs to the whole story.

On the same day on which I arrived at the clinic in Arlesheim, another person also arrived. She came from Silesia in Germany to attend the training course for nurses and curative teachers. She was a young children's nurse who, together with her sister, had started a small home for children with handicaps. Fräulein Maasberg was accommodated in the same boarding-house in which I had been given a room. We were led together, coming from two different parts of Europe, on the same day under the same roof.

I often met Fräulein Maasberg on the way to the clinic and she began to speak to me about her work and her family. We had a friendly relationship, but it was nothing very special. She returned to Silesia in February of the following year, but wrote me a letter inviting me to visit her school. She wanted me to see one of her sisters who was seriously ill and for whom, so she hoped, I would be able to do something.

Here again the motif of the sister appeared: first it was the funeral of Rudolf Steiner's sister which brought Ita Wegman to Vienna. Now it was Fräulein Maasberg's sister who made me visit her and her work. I accepted the invitation as in any case I had to lecture in Breslau which was very near.

One day before Ascension Day I arrived in Gnadenfrei, the little place which was the home of the Maasberg family. There for the first time in my life, I met the strong and very special aura of the *Herrnhuter Brüdergemeine,* the last offshoot of the Bohemian-Moravian Brotherhood. I first saw the ill sister and then was shown around. I walked through the graveyard up to the hill behind the village. I entered the church and saw the solemn and beautiful interior, the white pews, the majestic chandeliers, the offering-table, the pulpit of the minister. I was deeply moved by all the new experiences and a chord of my soul began to ring which I had never heard before. I met a sphere of my own destiny which had hitherto been unknown to me. As if in a dream, I walked through Gnadenfrei. Past and future merged with the present; images appeared and vanished again. I found myself within the living web of destiny and spiritual truth.

The same evening we drove to the school for children with handicaps which was situated a few miles further south, higher up in the Silesian mountains. It had been a day full of suspense and divination. I was quite unable at that time to grasp the meaning.

The following morning was Ascension Day. I was asked to speak to the children and to tell them something about this festival. I did so and in conclusion, played two pieces of Bach on the piano for them. I felt completely at ease and at home in the small house among the children and their helpers.

Herr Strohschein was the principal teacher in this school. He was one of the three young men who – at Christmas 1923 – had asked Rudolf Steiner to give some guidance for the work with children with handicaps. The answer was a lecture-course on educational therapy which Rudolf Steiner held during midsummer 1924. I was very glad to meet this man because I hoped to hear more from him about meetings and contacts he had had with Rudolf Steiner. In the course of our conversation, he asked me if I would consider joining him in this work. But my answer was, No. I told him that I imagined building up something bigger and that only if he would be able to find a much larger place, would I be willing to consider his proposal.

The same afternoon, a Herr and Frau von Jeetze visited the school. They were landowners who came from another part

Engraving of Schloss Pilgramshain

of Silesia not very far away. They had just decided to offer their large mansion house and park to the work for the handicapped children. They had actually come to ask if Fräulein Maasberg and Herr Strohschein would not consider renting their house. Here was the immediate answer to the proposal I had made a few hours before, I could hardly understand what was happening, but never before had I heard the stroke of the clock of destiny with such immediate power. I agreed at once to go to the new place as medical officer as soon as it would be opened.

On this very day, my dormant love for Fräulein Maasberg opened its wings and found faint approval. All this was still very tender and a subtle awakening-process. We hardly exchanged a word about this turn in our friendship, but somewhere, deep in our hearts, we knew of our common destiny. On the following day I left for Vienna where I visited my parents and from there I returned to Arlesheim and Dornach.

Work in Silesia

On Whit Monday, eleven days after the fateful Ascension Day, I delivered my second lecture at the Goetheanum. This time I was less successful. I felt a great deal of resistance and disapproval coming from the audience and this confirmed my decision to leave Dornach to take up my work in Silesia. Dr Wegman with whom I spoke about my plans was not at all agreeable to them. She had imagined that I would remain at her clinic for a number of years to help to build up the medical work there. I, however, knew that my place was with handicapped children.

The same year another sign of destiny was revealed to me. Together with Ita Wegman and some others, I travelled to London to attend the World Conference for Spiritual Science. The meetings were held at the Friends' House and were attended by a few hundred people. It was due to the initiative and enthusiasm of Ita Wegman that this conference had been arranged.

I again gave a lecture but had to speak in German for lack of knowing the English language sufficiently. My later friend, George Adams, translated the lecture and in him and many others, I met the English spirit for the first time. I visited Oxford and Cambridge, went to the British Museum and made several friends. During these days I was, of course, quite unaware, that within ten years time, I would be arriving in London as a refugee to settle down in Britain for good. Destiny tried to lift the veil for a moment's time, but I failed to recognise the meaning.

After the conference, Dr Wegman at last agreed to my change of place. With her approval, I went back to Arlesheim, packed my cases and travelled via Vienna to Silesia. I arrived in Pilgramshain at the beginning of September. This was the name of the new place we were to take over. A few friends had already begun to decorate the old house. They painted and

Albrecht Strohschein with his class in Pilgramshain

altered the rooms to make them ready to receive the first children. Fräulein Maasberg was also there. A few weeks later I proposed to her and she accepted.

The work grew considerably already during the first few months. Many children were sent to us especially from the children's department of the various districts of Berlin. We soon had between 70 and 80 handicapped and maladjusted boys and girls and had to learn how to deal with them.

On May 5, 1929, Fräulein Maasberg became Mrs König and we spent the first day of our honeymoon in Dresden where we saw Raphael's *Sistine Madonna*. From there we travelled to Prague and visited the famous castle of Karlstein. Then we went on to Vienna so that my parents could get to know my wife. I took the opportunity and paid a working-visit to the Institute of Embryology of the Vienna University where I had studied many years before.

Soon afterwards we returned to Pilgramshain where now years of hard work lay in front of us. More children found their way to our school and with them a great deal of responsibility was laid upon our shoulders. Herr Strohschein became the principal of the place and I was the medical officer. My wife gradually retired from the work after our first child was born. Two others followed in the course of the next years and gave her plenty to do in looking after them.

Meanwhile, my medical work increased and extended in a special way. Not hundreds, but thousand of patients came to consult me about their ills and troubles and there were days when I began at 8 am, only to have my supper at midnight. I became well-known as a physician throughout the whole of Silesia.

On top of the medical work, I regularly gave lectures in different towns of Germany. In the course of a few years my activities grew in every direction and became so manifold that I began to feel the stress and strain very strongly. I was gradually incapable of fulfilling all the demands put to me. I had hardly

König in his practice, Pilgramshain, 1929

any time left for personal studies and was unable to pursue my own path of research in the field of mental deficiency. At the same time, the political situation in Germany changed radically. In 1933, after Hitler had come to power, we began to feel the evil hand of this man and his political gang. There was no longer the intention nor the wish to help children in need of special care. Racial points of view became the idols of the great majority of the German people. In spite of my having been born Jewish and of not withholding the fact, my patients continued to consult me and instead of less, many more asked for advice and treatment.

My personal situation, however, became rather precarious. The Nuremberg Laws had come into effect and I could clearly see that the net was tightening around people who were not outspoken followers of the Nazi ideology. There was no future for myself and my children and I decided to look for work somewhere else in the world.

Beside the political pressure and instability, other signs pointed in the same direction. During the previous few years, human conditions in Pilgramshain had become very disappointing and I had already many times before contemplated leaving. Hardly any effort was made to create a real community among the members of the staff. On the contrary, there was constant discord and quarrel and my endeavours to overcome this lack of unity were in vain. I was especially dissatisfied with the economic arrangements concerning the coworkers. Time and again, I tried to remedy the situation but here, too, my efforts were thwarted.

All this made me decide to give up my work in Pilgramshain and to leave Germany altogether. Mrs König was wholeheartedly in tune with my decision as her high sense of morality and justice was deeply hurt by the conditions in and around Pilgramshain. We decided to move our family (now we had three children) to Vienna. There I intended to begin all over again as a medical practitioner.

Albrecht Strohschein, Walter-Johannes Stein (visiting), Karl König, Pilgramshain 1933

Before we left Germany, I wrote an open letter to the various Rudolf Steiner schools and homes for children with handicaps which had become established. In this letter, I stated my deep disappointment with the experiences I had had in Pilgramshain. And to myself I had to say: you have learned how such a school should *not* be run. Will you ever be able to do it better? Will you be able to build the hill?

This letter was written on February 27, 1936, on the seventy-fifth anniversary of Rudolf Steiner's birth. On March 7, my family and I left Germany with very mixed feelings. A new chapter in the search for the Candle on the Hill began.

Vienna again

In those days, one was not permitted to take any money out of Germany. I had, however, some friends in Austria who very kindly helped me to rent a house in one of the more fashionable suburbs of Vienna, so that I could commence with my medical work.

From Germany, we first went to Prague where we stayed with friends. We then spent a few weeks on the estate of another friend who was one of my patients. His country house was right in the heart of Bohemia quite close to the Castle of Karlstein. So here we were again at the place from whence we had started our first journey to Vienna. It was now seven years after our wedding.

We arrived in Vienna in the beginning of May and it was not easy to start work as a penniless medical practitioner. Quite a few weeks went by before the first patients found their way to my consulting-room and often my wife and I asked ourselves how we should altogether be able to carry on. With the approaching autumn, however, more ill people came to me and within a few months, I had so many patients that I needed an assistant or partner. Within one year's time, my waiting-room was filled to capacity throughout the day and the door of our house never stood still. Besides my medical work I gave weekly lectures to friends and patients. These talks were first held in our own house but soon we had to find a bigger room somewhere in the centre of Vienna. From 1937 on, between 100 and 200 people regularly attended these evenings. I spoke on many different subjects, mainly on certain aspects of anthropology and anthroposophy.

During this time, I was not very popular among the strict and dogmatic followers of Rudolf Steiner. I pursued my own way and did many things differently from what they thought right. I had the strong intention to make myself inwardly free from all kinds of sectarianism and to recreate Rudolf Steiner's ideas within myself. It was my conviction that he did not mean his pupils to merely repeat what he had once said, but they should rather become creative themselves. I have never intended to contradict this great man; yet I had certain doubts in some of the things he said and I tried to establish my own concepts and views. During these years I promised myself not to speak about anything for which I could not take full personal responsibility. For my lectures I chose only such subjects that I had properly studied and enlivened by my own point of view. I never imagined that I was not Rudolf Steiner's true pupil. My fundamental views were based on his philosophy and clairvoyant results, but I wanted to confirm these by personal studies and work. I had no desire to be only his mouthpiece. I demanded of myself that I represent my personally acquired ideas and views when I spoke and lectured.

Two to three times a month, there was a study-group for doctors and medical students that met in my house. Between 15 to 20 people attended these evenings. I usually gave an introductory talk about a special subject which was then followed by an all-round discussion. A number of interesting personalities were present and made some valuable contributions.

Among the medical students were a few who wished to know more about Rudolf Steiner and his work and they met together with other people in our youth group. Every Sunday evening 20 to 30 young friends came together. It had started with a small nucleus of about 8 to 10 students I had already known before I returned to Vienna. While I was in Pilgramshain, I visited my home-town once or twice a year to see my parents and to meet old friends. During these visits, I had become acquainted with this small group which was studying anthroposophy and whose members asked me to help them in their attempts to understand Rudolf Steiner's work. They were a closely-knit little community and deeply related to one another. A rather melancholic mood prevailed among them but they were earnestly striving young people.

To this nucleus, others soon attached themselves and a few months after I had arrived in Vienna, another closely-knit group of young people men and women appeared on the scene. They were just the opposite of the original band. They lived in style, enjoyed life and had a good amount of *savoir vivre*. Two of them, Peter Roth and Thomas Weihs, were in their last year of medical studies and others were around them. Carlo Pietzner was a graduate of art school, Alix Roth was working as a photographer, another was a musician and a few more were related to them. With this group, a fresh new wind blew through the *old* youth group and our evenings extended far into the night. We studied and read together, discussed the problems of the day, cultural and artistic as well as scientific. I was grateful to destiny for entrusting these outstanding representatives of the younger generation into my care and guidance.

For Christmas 1936 as well as 1937, we studied the Oberufer Christmas Plays together and performed them in the house of the Swedish Mission in Vienna. We began to like each other and to meet as often as our work would permit. During the year 1937, this youth group became a source of great satisfaction to me. I was able to mould a younger generation and lead them step by step to an understanding of the spiritual realities of the world.

In the course of this year, it became evident that we ought not only to study together but that we should in time do some common work. We expressed it in that we said: We do not want to read anthroposophy; we want to live it. We decided to aim at starting a home for children with handicaps: the candle on the hill began to appear again before my inner vision. Political conditions, however, pointed to another disaster. Hitler had already undermined the greater part of Austria with his fifth column and on the eve of 1937, I knew that the beginning of the end had come. When the spectacular northern lights appeared all over Europe on January 25, 1938, I again heard the knocking of destiny at my door. The clock of fate struck very audibly.

A few weeks later, Austria was occupied by the German army and the ruthless Nazi Party was in full power. A time of great tribulation, of pain and sorrow for tens of thousands of people followed. For us it was a time of testing and trial. Were we already strong enough to go steadfastly through this ordeal?

Finding a home in Scotland

On the evening of the occupation when the Austrian government had to resign and the new Nazi leaders assumed power, our youth group assembled. We read a lecture of Rudolf Steiner's together. It was one in which he speaks very powerfully of Michael the archangel,[2] and we were strengthened and reassured in turning to the words of our teacher.

A few days later, I went through a severe crisis. I realised that everything I had built up was again coming to an end. With the help of my wife, I quickly recovered my balance and turned my mind towards the future. It was obvious that we had to leave Austria and find again a new home somewhere else in the world.

Among most of my young friends the promise to live anthroposophy in common held fast. We began to plan for our exodus. First we thought we would go overseas, but I was against this idea. I saw the Second World War approaching as an inevitable event in the near future and I felt that we should not look for a refuge, but rather be somewhere near to where the catastrophes were going to happen. We first applied to the Irish Republic for permission to settle in or near Dublin, but our application was refused.[3] We then thought of going to Cyprus because entry to this island was still being granted. We soon dismissed the idea and came to the conclusion that each one of us should remain until the place where we would be able to begin our work could be found. We agreed to keep in close touch with one another and to give as much help as possible to those of us who needed it.

Week after week, one by one our group left; going to Italy and France, to Switzerland and Czechoslovakia, to Britain and Yugoslavia. It was as if in a last effort, we were to collect the whole of the European culture into our minds and hearts before uniting again. We entrusted ourselves to the unknown powers of the future and took the daring step of dispersing before coming together again.

My own way out of Austria was rather remarkable. During my last year in Vienna, I had become physician to the family of De Viti de Marco of Rome.[4] The two sisters, Lucia and Etta, frequently came to Vienna for treatment and became dear friends of our family. In these days of trial, Lucia appeared again and helped in every possible way to get me safely out of the country. My wife and I decided that she with our four children (the last was born in Vienna) should return to the home of her parents for the time being until I had found a place where we could once again be together.

Lucia came to Vienna with her car and on a beautiful Sunday morning in August of 1938 we left and in the evening of the same day after a severe trial with one of the passport officers, we crossed the border into Italy. I spent a few days with Lucia and Etta in their country house high up in the Apennine mountains.

The motif of the sister sounded again and this time very powerfully. It was the motif of the sisters that helped me to find the path, still veiled in the clouds of the future.

I travelled for a time between Switzerland and France, looking for the unknown place for our work. One day in October, when I was staying at the clinic in Arlesheim as the guest of Dr Wegman, she said to me, 'Why do you not try Scotland? I have friends near Aberdeen who may be willing to help you to start work there and to build up a new future.' I looked at her with great doubts and asked her if she knew how difficult it was to obtain an entry-permit for Britain. She dismissed these doubts and said something to the effect that if there is a will, the way ought to be found.

To my great astonishment two days later, I received a letter from the British Consulate in Bern saying that I and my family had been granted permission to enter the country and to settle down there permanently. It stated further that I was one of the selected group of 50 Austrian doctors permitted to study at one of the medical schools of the United Kingdom and to take the British medical degree. Now the die was cast.

I soon received my permit, discussed my immediate plans with Dr Wegman who furnished me with a letter of introduction to her friends, and then I went to Paris where I met up with Lucia de Viti. With her I arrived in London on December 8, 1938. The decisive step towards our goal was reached. The candle on the hill was faintly visible. Until this very day, I do not know for certain who it was who made the application to the British Home Office on my behalf. I had hardly ever contemplated settling down in Britain. My eyes were turned towards France or Switzerland. I can only guess that my great friend, the late Dr Eugen Kolisko, did it as silently as he had done so many other good things.[5]

A few days after my arrival in Britain, I travelled to Scotland and via Aberdeen reached the country estate of Williamston near Insch. Mr and Mrs Houghton, Dr Wegman's friends, received us

(I had travelled with Mr Roth, the father of Peter and Alix Roth) with very great kindness. They had already accepted one of the members of our youth group into their home as a permanent guest. Our hosts showed us over their house and estate. What a completely new world I encountered here! Everything seemed to be enchanted. The turmoil of the world was far away and the threat of the approaching war did not appear to exist. I still remember the old wild ducks which had settled down on a pond in the beautiful garden of Williamston, a symbol of peace and remoteness. The Houghtons invited my wife and children to come and stay with them after Christmas and they also showed me a house, an empty old manse, quite near to their own house which they proposed to acquire for us and to adapt so that we could start with our work as soon as possible. This was more than I had hoped to achieve in so short a time. Here was a house, a roof under which we could begin! My family would be with me again in a few weeks' time! My friends would be called together and would soon be reunited.

I hurried back to London and wrote a Christmas letter, full of hope and promise to all my people. Mrs König arrived with our children on December 30, and on the pier at Harwich stood the faithful Lucia at my side, waiting to welcome the precious freight.

Beginnings in Camphill

In the first days of the year 1939, I accompanied my family to Williamston to introduce them to Mr and Mrs Houghton. I showed our prospective home to my wife and we discussed the rearrangements in and around the old manse. The place was called Kirkton House. We were both extremely happy at this turn of events and were looking forward very eagerly to our new start in life. We decided that we should try and begin with the work by the end of March.

On my return journey to London, I called at Dundee and presented myself to the dean of the medical school there. He very kindly accepted me as an advanced student at St Andrew's University. I also stayed in Edinburgh for a few days to negotiate with the Scottish Christian Council for Refugees which the Church of Scotland had set up. I remember the great understanding and help I received there from the Reverend Macanna.

Back to London, one of my main tasks was the endless visits to Bloomsbury House where innumerable Refugees Committees sat at work. I also went to the Home Office several times and spoke to the different departments there about my plans to start a home for children with handicaps. All this was done in order to obtain the entry permits for all my young friends. I was met with great friendliness but with little understanding. In the end I won the battle. I was given an overall permit allowing 15 coworkers to enter Great Britain. This was just the appropriate number to cover our needs.

On March 30, 1939, fourteen years after Rudolf Steiner's death, Mrs König, together with Alix Roth and Ann Nederhoed, Peter Roth's wife, moved to Kirkton House. On the same day Peter Roth and I left London for Edinburgh and after several meetings with refugee organisations, we arrived at Kirkton House on April 1. Every Monday morning I travelled to Dundee to the medical school, returning to Kirkton House at the weekends. The new work began. We now started to dig the foundations for the hill on which the candle was to stand. Within a few weeks' time, the first children were admitted. In the course of the ensuing months, my young friends began to arrive one by one from Europe. The clouds of the oncoming war gradually drew nearer and just before it broke out, the last of our number joined us. We were together again – in a foreign country at the brink of a terrible war – a tiny company of shipwrecked people in a nutshell of a boat.

We had never before lived so closely together. We began

The pioneers at Kirkton House 1939
(Tilla König is fourth from the right)

to know one another more intimately and to find out what it is like to work in common. To every one of us, this meant a period of complete adjustment. We went through many ups and downs together and each single day, a new trial had to be gone through.

Our relationship to the Houghtons became increasingly difficult. The barriers of language and nationality were very deep; we were regarded as foreigners, something like natives who had to do what they were told. We, however, wanted to be our own agents and to build up our work according to our own ideas. The demand for the admittance of children rose steadily and so we soon began to look for a new house, more spacious, nearer to the city of Aberdeen and further away from Williamston.

With the help of Mr W.F. Macmillan who wished his son to become one of our pupils, we were able to acquire the estate of Camphill.[6] This was a decisive step forward. But suddenly another big hurdle appeared in front of us. We had arranged to move from Kirkton House to the new place at the end of May, 1940. On Whitsunday, May 12, the police suddenly came and

Camphill House in wartime

interned all the men. We were first taken to Banff and after two weeks moved on to Liverpool. Had everything come to an end? What were our women going to do? Would they dare to move to Camphill? Were we men going to be interned for the rest of the war?

Many rumours swept through the camp; we were all going to be shipped to Canada, to Australia, to South Africa. All our women had also been interned. The Germans had started to invade Britain, and so on, and so on …

We few friends were very fortunate in being allowed to remain together. We began to read and to do some common work. Later on, we were removed to the Isle of Man and it was there that a spirit of community began to grow in our hearts. Meanwhile, we heard from our women that they had decided to leave Kirkton House and move to Camphill on the planned day of entry. They arrived there on June 1. To us who were interned, this was a great encouragement. This bold step gave us the reassurance that our work would continue. At the same time, some of our British friends tried to obtain our release

In the gardens of Camphill (Photograph by Edith Tudor Hart)

from internment. At this fateful time, during the months of August and September, the Battle of Britain which saved the country from the invasion was fought.

I was released from the camp on October 4, 1940, and travelled back to Camphill. My joy was great. Here was the place on which the hill would be built, here were the friends to help, here were the first children in need of special care, here was the foundation for making our dreams and ideals come true. Within a few months, all my friends had returned from internment and the work really began. Each week, we built up another part of the hill and it slowly began to rise before our eyes. A great amount of labour, of trial and error, of sorrow and happiness has gone into this building.

For a few years now, the candle is burning on top of the hill and many children have seen its light and have come to live in its radiance. The experience of the first Advent Sunday thirty-three years past was a seed; out of it, a tree began to grow the stem of which rooted in Camphill, but its branches spread far and wide.

I have just finished these last sentences which conclude the story of Camphill. Today is February 27, 1961, the centenary of Rudolf Steiner's birth. I am on board a ship in the southern Atlantic, bound for South Africa. My heart is filled with reverence and gratitude to my destiny which has led me to work in the name of this great man.

Karl König on the ship to South Africa, 1961

Three Stars, Pillars and Essentials

Contemplations about Karl König's Essays on the Camphill movement

Richard Steel

Eighty years after the 'birth moment' – or at least one of those moments – of Camphill, on March 11, 1938 in Vienna, which was followed by Karl König's journey as refugee to Britain, it seems important to look at the various milestones placed by König himself during the pioneering stages of the Camphill movement; essays he wrote to describe how the anthroposophical ideals and impulses were finding their outer expression in social life, in the 'social experiment' as he called it at the end of the Village Conferences.[1] Indeed it is time now to revisit these essays in their context in order to give them their central place within this volume of inner Camphill history.

The essays were written between 1959 and 1965, and clearly build upon each other. Nevertheless the only one to be reprinted in more recent years was the third, 'The Three Essentials,' which reappeared in 2003 as an appendix to *A Sense for Community*, a wide-ranging examination of the Camphill movement authored by Michael and Jane Luxford, and also in 2010 in Jan Bang's *A Portrait of Camphill*, a renewed edition of *A Candle on the Hill* (Cornelius Pietzner's book with many photographs published in 1990 to mark fifty years of the movement). In this last compilation the essay was embedded in an article by Christof-Andreas Lindenberg, and within the narrative a part of the first essay ('The Three Stars') was also included. In the present volume all three essays are placed into their context – a series of three steps, defining the first 25 years of Camphill.

For many years, particularly within Camphill circles, the first two essays were actually better known and often quoted. 'The Three Stars of the Camphill Movement' and 'The Three Pillars of the Camphill Movement' were printed in a little booklet edited by Anke Weihs called *The Camphill Movement* which enjoyed a number of print runs and translation into various languages. It was given to all and sundry who came into contact with Camphill, whether as co-workers, parents or social workers, since it gave a description of the spiritual background and striving of the communities. The 'Three Essentials of the Camphill Movement' continues the theme, as indicated already by the title, but very much out of the position König was in during that year (1965) – in the pioneering situation of Camphill in Germany. He had just moved back to Central Europe, having withdrawn from leadership of the whole movement to take on this newly emerging region. The countries where Camphill was beginning to set foot – Germany, Switzerland and Holland (at that time still belonging to the Irish region!) – had legal settings which made necessary a wage system, taxation and social security. This was a new challenge for Camphill, moving back into a Europe which was remodelling itself after the war. It meant that new forms and social processes were going to be needed.

From stars to pillars

The first essay of this series, 'The Three Stars of the Camphill Movement,' was written in 1959 by Karl König to commemorate twenty-one years since his arrival in Britain. In a way we can see how König here began with the stars, with high ideals which he had shared with his youth group in Vienna; spiritual impulses setting out on their way to realisation. 'Stars' is a wonderful term because firstly it reminds us of our heavenly origin, where we are connected to tasks of destiny and needs of the world; but secondly it indicates how something of a spiritual nature can be a guiding principle, shining above and beyond earthly deeds and accomplishments. Naming three personalities in this context should not be confused with making such personalities into (pop)stars, but striving to see their intentions and spiritual impulses – especially those which they were unable to realise during their lives. At the end of the first essay König even likens these three, Comenius, Zinzendorf and Owen, to the three kings, offering their gifts for the future of humanity.

This was a consistent continuation of the method Karl König had used with the youth group in Vienna – asking each member to concern themselves with a personality who had died young during the First World War, unable to fulfil their destiny. Later, the same approach appeared in a special way as König gave tasks to groups among the committed members of the Camphill community. Here also historical personalities were chosen. Morwenna Bucknall told me about the evening when he 'dealt out' these patrons for the group work: she was 'allotted' the social reformer Robert Owen. He was not new to her; her father was an early British socialist, and at that time Owen was basically only known in those circles or by ardent students of Rudolf Steiner, who had written about Owen's early social endeavours and particularly about his failings (the context of which will be discussed later). Morwenna was horrified after her friends had been given wonderful personalities like Joan of Arc, Rembrandt and Iphigenia, and couldn't help but ask outright, 'Owen? What can he do for us?' König, as might be expected, thundered his reprimand, 'It is not a question of what *he* can do for *us*, but of what *we* can do for *him!*' Attention to historical figures did not imply developing any personality cults, but rather discerning spiritual impulses and how they have manifested in history, in order to further them in a modern context. Certainly the significance for Camphill of Owen, Comenius and Zinzendorf can be understood only in that way.

The second essay, 'The Three Pillars of the Camphill Movement', was written a year later, 1960, in time for the twenty-first birthday of Camphill, which was simultaneously the beginning of planning for the first Camphill Hall – a milestone in the 'incarnation' of the original impulse. Thus also the image of architectural pillars, supporting the roof of the growing movement. Here are described the three structural 'building elements' of Camphill: the college meeting, the Bible Evening and the fundamental social law in their connection to the inner motifs of the three 'stars'.

These two essays were then printed in the booklet *The Camphill Movement* – as a gift for the many friends of Camphill on its twenty-first birthday, to show them what ideals had been leading and forming this movement. At the end of her preface, Anke Weihs wrote the following words, obviously significant for understanding the context in which the essays were written and used:

> As we shall soon go on into a new period of life and work, we hope that it may be given to us to continue our attempts to mould and bring to living existence the ideals that have led us so far.

It was clear to those around Karl König that they always had to reconnect with their spiritual aims and ideals so that these might find suitable expression and development according to the needs and circumstances of the world, and at the same time in concord with the community's growing and changing biography. Such a process needed continual and fully conscious reviewing.

For many years this little booklet with the first two essays was given to all new co-workers across the world. Then that was discontinued, the realisation having arisen that Camphill as a movement had become so diverse and had moved on so far that these essays would need to be embedded in some further narrative, or at least properly introduced. Actually a *fourth* essay would have needed to be written in order to continue the sequence. This was in the 1980s, but at the time no-one managed to do it. The physician Hans Müller-Wiedemann wanted to take on the task but needed first to finish the König biography, which he managed for 1992. Subsequent years of illness and then his death in 1997 prevented him from continuing his writing in the name of his friend and teacher Karl König.

The third essay – essentials

The third essay, 'The Three Essentials of the Camphill Movement,' was written as an editorial for *The Cresset,* the then journal of the Camphill movement, for Michaelmas 1965 – to celebrate 25 years of Camphill. It is clear from the historical background, but also in Karl König's choice of title, that this was a continuation, a renewed observation of the developing movement. The very word 'movement' indeed implies an entity which is living, changing and progressing.

A German translation was soon undertaken – König himself was after all back in the country of his own native tongue – but it was only published in 1966, after his death, along with a second essay he had written for *Das Seelenpflege-bedürftige Kind* the German curative journal of that time. One should also note here that on his return to Central Europe König had attempted from the start to mend various rifts between Camphill and other anthroposophical institutions, many of which were in German-speaking countries. So his new position in Germany gave cause for new publications. The two German-language essays were now to be presented in a booklet called *Living and Working in Camphill*. And since this was to go far outside internal Camphill circles, König realised that a revision would be necessary.

However, he did not get round to it, and we only know of a remark he made to Georg von Arnim, as quoted in the preface of the booklet, about a need to revise it. The only change König had indicated was at the beginning of the second section, where the question comes in of the difference between Camphill and other institutions. He wanted that cut out because it was actually unfair to others (especially to other anthroposophical institutions, and also was in their case not quite true.) The relevant sentences were excluded in later use, and for translation purposes. Probably König would already then have also changed the part in the third section about paid work, which could well have been seen as a provocative remark about the quality of Camphill in comparison to other communities, but also in its brief form could be seen as too restrictive, holding on to the wisdom of forms valid at that time but leaving little room for developments.

Fixed conservatism was not at all König's style, he being the very person who would again and again make sweeping changes within the young community, so much so that some of its members often worried about losing elements they had just got used to. There never really was such a strong contrast between Camphill and many other anthroposophical centres on the Continent, but there was still tension over the fact that König had left Pilgramshain partly because of his social striving which was not shared by all others, whereas he understood this to be of great importance to Ita Wegman as leader of the Medical Section.[2]

Georg von Arnim was Karl König's physician during his last years, and talked to him specifically about publications. Later he edited a number of König's essays, including the well-known ones about the lower senses, always putting them into context and continuing the research which had been important to König – on this level they worked well together, von Arnim too being a passionate researcher. They also shared concerns about social life, social threefolding and the fundamental social law. When publishing the 'Three Essentials' (along with the other essay), von Arnim wrote in his preface: 'Karl König was not really satisfied with the way he had expressed himself in that essay and wanted to rework it before publication, but unfortunately did not manage this due to his early death.'

The added essay written for the German journal balanced some things out. But certainly the essays about the 'Stars' and 'Pillars' are much wider and more general, and their context shows how the three principles can be used and adapted to any situation; the 'Three Essentials' does just that, seeing those principles in a specific situation. The later essay is not a reworking of the previous two as an overriding manual of guidance. Reading the series of three essays gives a very different picture. It is maybe unfortunate that König used the word 'essentials', which seems to imply that this essay defines what Camphill is or isn't meant to be. Perhaps help may be found by comparing the use of the word 'essential' for ethereal oils, as the very essence of specific substances, extracted from their living context and presenting their essential nature. 'Essentials' were certainly not meant as a directive for how Camphill should be defined in the future; that would not have been in keeping with the form of König's essays, nor indeed with his Memoranda, of which there were also three. (He spoke of a 'sphere of the Fourth Memorandum', although he never actually wrote one.) The Memoranda were written in 1945, 1948 and 1951, describing details of tasks and community forms. During the Holy Nights of 1950/51 when the Third Memorandum was decided upon, König wrote a letter in order to stress the significance of young people and the newly formed Camphill Youth Group, and here stated the following:

> If the past is to be a measure for the community – for example if ten years' membership leads a person to think: I can do this or that, or I have the right to do this or that – it is wrong. And even the holding of a position in the Community means nothing if older members are not willing to walk with the stream of development

in the Community ... Some are there to stand behind and remain occupied with what was once necessary for the Community, because if every one of us would run ahead, we should lose all. There is the period of the First Memorandum, the period of the Second Memorandum, the period of the Third Memorandum. Not all of us have the task to go on, but all those who have the task to remain behind should know it and they should be able to remain behind ... but not holding back those who want to walk forward.

The third star or pillar and the fundamental social law

Karl König might not be too happy if words he had written fifty years ago in the context of a particular situation were taken up without inquiring into how such matters might need to be re-conceived today. We know that he constantly revised and metamorphosed Camphill's life and work, so that its original impulses were re-enlivened and it continued to evolve. His various essays and Memoranda reflect this ongoing change. Since his death the question has naturally arisen of how to continue in this respect, without either letting things drift the way they will under extraneous and sometimes quite different currents (inertia of the heart, he might have called it), or holding on to old things and ways which some like to call the Camphill ethos, whatever that may denote. I like to think of a statement by König's favourite composer, Gustav Mahler, 'Tradition is to nurture the flame, not to worship the ashes.'

Questions are of course now being raised about all three historical 'expressions' of the essentials. The college meeting has found various new forms in different places and within other cultures; the Bible Evening also. If we look back to the 'Stars' we can find a similar metamorphosis into present situations.

There is a special difficulty regarding the third essential, as expressed in König's statement:

> It is remuneration, not money, that creates a barrier between the one who gives and the one who receives. Giving and receiving is a matter of reciprocal human relationships; the genuine relationship vanishes as soon as remuneration intervenes. The service of sacrifice cannot be paid, because paid love is no love; paid help no longer has anything to do with real help.

One may well wonder whether these characteristically incisive and undeniably thought-provoking statements might nonetheless have been among those which König wanted to reconsider and revise at the time of his death in 1966. Would he speak or write in the same tone and with the same words today, when the reality – for various reasons – is that throughout many Camphill centres around the world wages are now being paid? Might he not find another way of expressing what lives in the relevant ideal so that it was not formulated as such a divisive absolute and could also embrace the service, love and help which surely also stream through the work of many co-workers and employees receiving wages? How do we continue to find the 'essence' of this ideal?

Here is perhaps one of the greatest challenges for Camphill in the twenty-first century, touching on manifold current problems faced by society all around us. Finding the meaning of work and appropriate forms of remuneration is an important task for humanity in our new millennium. It cannot be the task of the present publication to explore such issues further. But it seems to belong in a special way to König's destiny that at the end of his life he was chairman of Camphill's Central European Region, the very one which a short time later was accused of leaving the path of Camphill by searching for new ways to work with regulations governing labour and wages. We need to remember that in these essays König was *describing* the forms evolved out of circumstances of general society which Camphill was trying to serve and out of community substance which had developed for that purpose, not *prescribing* how things should be in the future. In fact he repeatedly said that he did not know how things would develop, and begged his listeners to be aware and observe for themselves.

Although there has been continued work on the theme of the fundamental social law within Camphill, in future this will certainly have to increase, in accordance with the dimension perceived by Rudolf Steiner. As he stated in a lecture in 1905:

> We want to firm up the soul through the law of its own inner being, so that it learns to place its powers at the disposal of the whole from points of view other than the law of wages and self-interest ... Thus labour becomes anything but a burden. It becomes something into which we place what is most sacred for us, our compassion for humanity, and then we can say: Labour is sacred because it is a sacrifice for mankind.[3]

Yes indeed, this third star or pillar is far-reaching and has particularly to do with inner development and esoteric work, not just with methods of distributing pocket money and avoiding taxes. König knew from Rudolf Steiner that any step in spiritual development has to be accompanied by two steps in moral development.

The fundamental social law: living the future

The research which would be necessary on the fundamental social law is admittedly rather daunting, because here we are looking far into the future and can realise that this area needs the most flexibility, the most imaginative experimentation: it has to do with the economic sphere which will only become fully conscious to the human race in the sixth cultural epoch. The earlier oriental epochs formed out spiritual life; the Greco-Roman epoch brought social and political life into consciousness; and now we are living at a time when economics sets the conditions for society but out of unconscious, therefore mostly egoistic, impulses (which is actually *not* a contradiction). Economic forms of today still follow patterns used by the Celts.

It was Carlo Pietzner whom Karl König called to carry conscience and responsibility for the economic life of Camphill, starting already during his early years there. Why ask an artist? And was there a connection between this and the fact that Carlo Pietzner was also sent westwards – first to Ireland (where Celtic traditions had lived on to unite with an esoteric Christianity) and then to the United States? The drive to understand the economic realm was a fundamental striving throughout Carlo's Camphill life.[4] He stressed that bringing a penetrating understanding to this realm was a primary task for Camphill in America, because Ahrimanic forces work most strongly there into and through economic activity. And many times he emphasised something which may be expressed thus: 'Do not project Ahrimanic forces onto others or different groups of people in society. You must learn to recognise them in yourselves, and work to transform them.'

Economic life is a key to the future. Although we do not yet really know what brotherliness fully involves, we can at least open the way towards finding out. This task belongs to the American continent in particular, and König clearly met it there. Transformation of the economic realm is directly tied up with the interrelationships between human beings working together and for each other – whether they know it or not.

We are looking particularly at two of the three realms: reimbursement belongs to the economic, and work to the middle realm. And a 'law' – even a spiritual one – anyway belongs to the sphere of rights. These two realms are in our times still intertwined. The question is how to free up work so that it does not become a commodity, and so that working *out of* our karma and working *with* the karma of others stands in its own right between spiritual aims and economic processes.

In this context I would like to quote again from the letter written by Karl König to Community Members in 1948, which we have looked at in the Introduction. It became known as the Second Memorandum:

> The institutions in Camphill have come about through the fact that anthroposophy ... has lightened up in the souls of the members or through the fact that the Community itself has been experienced by newcomers as an ideal to which they desire to devote themselves ... But now people have entered these institutions who, for instance, do not meet the Community with sufficient understanding; or also people who gladly accept the forms of life of the Community but are not sufficiently close to anthroposophy because their souls are not so constituted that they are able to accept it ... With this the Community is given a special task, the fulfilment of which requires much tact and insight, for the institutions must be there for all people, but not the Community. The Community must maintain a wakeful eye for the institutions it brings about and it must serve those people who wish to live in its atmosphere.

It can be seen that the question had henceforward to be faced – and was often voiced by König – of how the Community would stand in relation to the movement (in 1948 not yet a concept) and how the former might imbue the latter with spiritual impulses while at the same time developing 'much tact'. And so often it is especially monetary questions – even amongst spiritually striving people – which can lead unwittingly to tactlessness.

To live in intentional community today is to practice something that will only really be possible in the future, but actually to live the future in the present moment is of course impossible, therefore at best very difficult! But this has always been the task of mystery centres, and today we are potentially *all* involved in new mysteries.

Rudolf Steiner's essays

Rudolf Steiner had also written three essays which we have as basis for our studies of the fundamental social law; they are just a fragment, since he did not continue them as planned: there was too little interest amongst the (then) theosophical friends.[5] These essays, however, explain that there are three layers to the question of the fundamental social law, and it is as though all three 'layers' are again mirrored within the economic realm. Firstly there is the question of a common mission (independent cultural/spiritual life) which is a precondition for any social entity. Then exact steps are described towards a recognition of karma (sphere of rights). And finally Steiner discusses the institution of forms which allow human beings to separate work from economic processes. His explanations make quite clear that this is why Robert Owen could not fulfil his impulse of social reform – what he created was only an institution of economic life, without the other two spheres. In addition Steiner introduces a fourth factor, namely that it was not yet possible for Owen to reckon with the development of the individual self or 'I', which stands as a magical fourth layer penetrating these three spheres: 'All this is only possible if the people involved find their way out of egoism' – to their true 'I'.

So we can see that Rudolf Steiner introduced his threefold principles on the level of individual development. At the same time as he wrote his series of essays, he also gave an esoteric lesson as well as a public lecture about the same subject.[6] Later the political situation demanded presenting threefolding on a macro-social level. That would be a theme of its own; may it suffice here to indicate how, after the failure of the threefold movement on a political, national and international level, he returned in his lectures to the micro-social level – how the individual can prepare a threefold approach as an inner schooling. Carlo Pietzner's favourite lectures, *Spiritual Science as a Foundation for Social Forms,* belong to this series, as do the lectures *The Bridge between Universal Spirituality and the Physical,* and for instance the Youth Course, *Youth and the Etheric Heart,* which was so important for the preparation of the Camphill founders back in the Vienna youth group.

There is of course always an institutional or 'meso-social' aspect to threefolding and social 'laws' such as the fundamental social law. This is something which in a way succeeded: Steiner was able to found the Waldorf School out of the threefold movement. Communities created by Camphill also belong to this level – as a link between the development of an individual and the re-creation of society. Rudolf Steiner, as well as Karl König, created social organisms because they are needed, not because they are profitable. To use an obvious example: the care given to people in Camphill will hopefully always be given because it is needed in order to uphold their true humanity, not because it brings in a profit! The income of individuals doing the work is unrelated to the work, but is related to their needs. I think that is the level we need to be addressing today. It relieves an individual from undue pressure, and connects to the question of the 'common mission' as described in Steiner's essays. These make clear the intention of developing the 'I', which is a major task. Camphill communities, like Waldorf schools, are social entities with a huge task for the future – that of enabling proper growth for the human 'I'.

A fourth essay?

Finally we can ask the question: how would a *fourth* essay look today? After the death of Karl König and subsequent advances in social work and in paradigms of integration and inclusion, one can see a steady shift within the Camphill movement, with its increasing diversity and its own integration in many countries into the social and sometimes political field. This shift is one away from more homogeneous, secluded and almost sectarian life-sharing communities with strong internal structures as well as personal devotion and personal sacrifice, centred around curative education and the relatively new task of social therapy. It takes place *parallel* to advances in general society – advances often accompanied by all the downfalls and exaggerations which we know only too well – but also quietly and selflessly. Such advances indeed were often unconsciously initiated and nurtured by Camphill's presence especially over the second half of the twentieth century leading up towards a new millennium.

In his 'History of Curative Education' and particularly in his forward-looking essay of the same period (1965) on 'The Purpose and Value of Curative-Educational Work'[7] König demonstrates the parallelism of societal development (and its problems) with the arising and unfolding of curative work. Again, one can appreciate that Camphill has contributed to general developments in society, without forgetting that it was never alone – neither in social reforms, nor in curative education, nor in working with anthroposophy. Camphill always belonged, and still belongs, intrinsically to the working of the Spirit of our Time. In this context the ultimate task of any social entity or community today will be to further the realisation of the true self, searching for its proper place in the world.

In the same year as the third essay was written, 1965, König produced that profound article just mentioned, 'The Purpose and Value of Curative-Educational Work'. Its central part reads as follows:

An affluent society that is about to forget its humanity; a society that becomes deeply involved in its racial problems and at the same time has made weapons that can destroy millions of people in a few minutes; a society that has forgotten the divine order is seeking new ethics which it cannot find in a state of godlessness; such a society brings about a new set of tasks: to support those who are disabled, timid, lame and ailing in such a way that they can reclaim their humanity.

Is it not a great miracle that wants to manifest itself here? A self-destructive humanity creates within itself something new like a fresh bud within the dying part of its existence. A comprehensive curative education is like the developing seed inside a rotting fruit.

We only need to define the concept of curative education widely enough to see its true purpose … Its intention is to become a global task to help counteract the 'threat to the individual person' which has arisen everywhere. The 'curative-educational attitude' needs to express itself in any social work, in pastoral care, in the care for the elderly, in the rehabilitation of mentally ill and physically handicapped people, in the guidance of orphans and refugees, of suicidal and desperate individuals, in the international Peace Corps and similar ambitions.

This is the only answer we have today – inasmuch as we still want to be human beings – for a society dancing on the brink of disaster …

Only support from person to person – the encounter of a self with another self – the awareness of another individuality without questioning the other's religion, convictions and political background – just the gaze from eye to eye between two personalities, creates the kind of curative education which can, in a healing way, counteract the threat to the core of humanity.[8]

Looking from our present perspective we can perhaps remember that Camphill began in its first years without regular financing, without job descriptions, often without any specific training. Every last bit of time and energy went into pioneering a curative community, an individual co-worker for instance sleeping in a room with up to eight children who often needed attention even at night: a situation which in most cases we cannot and should not want to repeat! But first and foremost these co-workers experienced the necessity of taking their development and destiny into their own hands, even though the younger ones were far from an understanding of anthroposophy, many also coming from a non-Christian background.

Our present world shows us itself that Karl König's deliberations still need to be taken with the uttermost seriousness. The very forms of society today call for healing and transforming, right down to the details of employment regulations, wages and insurances, division of work and responsibilities. And intertwined with all these practicalities is the deep underlying question: how can more and more people, subject to the outer constraints of the modern 'care industry', experience therein the *real* basis for their work – reincarnation and karma? In the past that has been divined by so many who strove to share lives with and assist people with special needs, but according to Rudolf Steiner this becomes especially hidden by the payment of wages. This makes the question both more difficult to answer but also more insistent within a modern economic context. For the urgent need of our time is to know where one's *real* origin is. Anthroposophy is not meant just for little groups which become self-contained and self-righteous, but to be opened up to any persons in the world who wish to receive it, and thus to become a light for the whole of society. Is not this social therapy, a healing of social life itself, a new path of Christianity?

And to end with one may also ask: what suitable image could now be found to add to the stars, pillars and essentials? Readers must ponder that question for themselves and come up with their own answers. The aim of the present contribution is to suggest that such a question could be newly addressed by studying these three essays – the legacy we have inherited from König himself. It seems to be a need which strongly presents itself 77 years down the road from the founder women's move into Camphill Estate. The necessity still arises today of assessing the present situation of Camphill in the spiritually true and future-oriented way which König achieved in his three essays, written at pivotal points of his own life as well as of Camphill's unfolding biography.

The Three Stars of the Camphill Movement

Inklings of a new beginning

Christmas 1959 – and it is twenty-one years ago that I first celebrated this festival here in Britain and not in my own country. I was sitting in a tiny room, in one of the hundreds of back streets of London. alone, a drop in that human sea of a city, a stranger, a foreigner. I knew that together with me, tens of thousands of people shared the same fate. Men and women, old and young, children and adults, we were uprooted from the native soil and saved, like a plant which is given a handful of earth in a little pot of clay. How would we survive?

The small candle in front of me lit the few green branches on he mantelpiece and the gas fire hummed a low song. My thoughts went out into the future. Would it be possible to turn this lonely life into order and shape again? Would the fragments of my existence be put together again so that they may form a new frame? I was one of the many who were just too young to be a soldier in the First World War. Then came a time of breathtaking recovery and all seemed to be well when, gradually, a second war appeared on the horizon. And here I was, thrown out of my work and I felt like one, who after a shipwreck, was cast on a lonely, unknown island.

The flame of the candle jerked and quivered and threw strange shadows on the wall. I had left Europe behind me. London was no longer the land of Europe; it was a country of

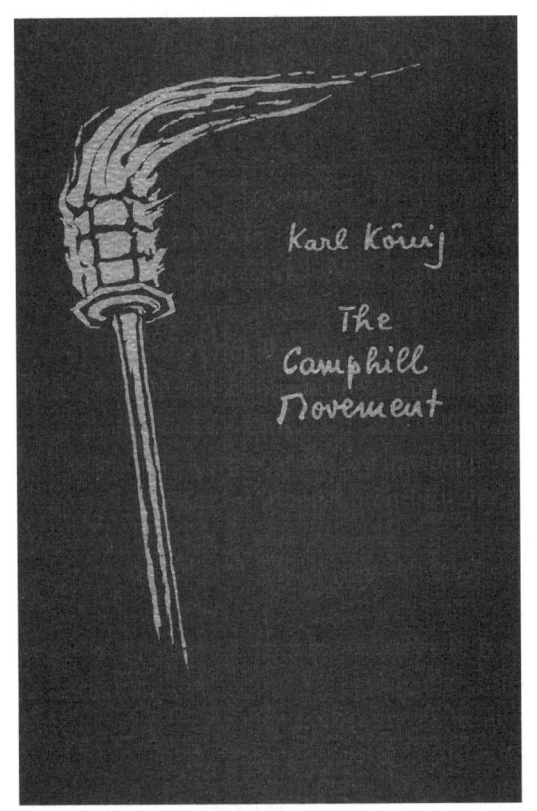

Cover of booklet The Camphill Movement *printed in 1961, containing this and the following essay, 'The Three Pillars of the Camphill Movement'.*

the western world. The language was foreign to me; the people were strangers; their way of living was not my way and their past was almost unknown to me. I had a different background, different modes of existence, different thoughts. Some of these strangers had turned to me with a friendly gesture. Others, on whom I had previously counted, showed no more interest than the limits of good behaviour would permit.

I was alone! Would I again have the strength to begin anew? In a few days my wife and children were to arrive and, in several countries of the Continent, a number of young friends were waiting to join me. Join me in what? Would I be permitted to work? And if so, what kind of work was I to do? But in Italy and France, in Holland and Switzerland, in Germany and Czechoslovakia friends were waiting to join me. A house had been found in the north of Scotland, where we could start to live together, but what kind of life would we live? It would only be an enclave in this land; we would be strangers in a big community. And what was our task to be?

The light of the candle now was quiet and bright and my eyes turned to a small book which a kind person had given me as a Christmas present. It was an English Bible; never before had I held one in my hands. I was astonished to realise that the present translation was sponsored by James I, a man and monarch, for whom for many years I had had the highest esteem. I had learned to admire this 'wisest fool of Christendom' and I now read the following words in the dedication: 'to go forward with the confidence and resolution of a Man in maintaining the truth of Christ, and propagating it far and near.' Is this not a common ground on which I may stand, I asked myself.

It was common ground. And now I saw and knew more about the future task which lay before me. I saw Austria overrun and conquered by men who had betrayed the very essence of the destiny of Europe. They had turned it in a camp of nationalists, searching for might and power. Europe was overcome by their vain glory and was preparing to become a battlefield. Could we not take a morsel of the true European destiny and make it into a seed so that some of its real task might be preserved: a piece of its humanity, of its inner freedom, of its longing for peace, of its dignity?

If this were possible, would it not be worthwhile to live and work again? Let us begin to become a morsel of this Europe which, at the moment, has to disappear. But let us not do it in words but in deeds, to serve and not to rule, to help and not to force; to love and not to harm. This would be our task. Thus I was thinking.

I understood my thoughts. They had emerged after weeks of trial and need and now stood before me and helped me to clarify my problem of existence. On this Christmas Eve neither Camphill nor the movement existed. The future was shrouded but a will started to find its way.

Symbiosis

There was, from the beginning, a task which we had set before us: curative education. Some of us were trained in this work and the rest were willing to grow into it. We felt it as a special kind of mission to bring this work about. We had learned from Rudolf Steiner a new understanding of the child with handicaps and we had seen this work in several homes and schools on the Continent and in Great Britain. To add another place to those already existing, was our first goal.

At the same time, we dimly felt that at that time children with handicaps were in a position similar to ours. They were refugees from a society which did not want to accept them as part of their community. We were political refugees, these children social refugees.

The symbiosis between them and us seemed to work very well. Already the first children, who were given into our care, felt quite at home with us and we had no difficulties in accepting them fully and wholeheartedly in our midst. They gave us the work which we wanted to do; they provided us with the conviction that we fulfilled a necessary task and were not superfluous and useless members of this country. Through the children we were able to earn our livelihood and not be dependent on public help and charity. The most important fact was, however, that these children demanded of us a special way of life. It was not only up to us to educate and train them; it was they, also through the simple fact of their special existence, who asked of us qualities which we had to develop. They asked for patience, equanimity and compassion. They asked for an understanding of their particular ways and behaviour. Every day was for us an new trial in humanity and self-education. It was a tremendous opportunity which had been given into our hands.

At the same time we had to learn to care for the grounds and the garden, to look after the house, to do the cooking and all the other domestic work, as we, from the very beginning, had decided not to employ any staff or servants, but to do all the work with our own hands. We used this work as one of the means of curative education and the children, in so far as they could manage, helped with every domestic task.

Our own children became part of the whole house-community and, in this way, the supposed barriers between mentally disabled and ordinary children were completely abolished. It was, to many of us, a revelation to see how *normal* children with handicaps were. Day after day the whole field of curative education assumed a completely new form of approach. We realised the need of these children to be accepted into a closed social surrounding which, on the one side, would provide for them a sheltered environment and, on the other, the possibility to unfold their individual qualities.

Gradually we grew aware of the necessity and the strong and urgent claim made upon us to undergo an inner training in self-knowledge and self-recognition. Rudolf Steiner's books and lecture provided us with the necessary advice and from there we drew our guidance. We discovered furthermore, that for the children as well as for us a deeply religious life was a need. The observation of the festivals, the recognition of the Sunday, the common prayer for the whole house-community in the morning as well as in the evening, grew to be an indispensable factor. We observed how the ordering of the day helped our children and gave them an inner hold. It supported us also in our effort to become our own masters.

In this way, a closely knit fabric of human relations developed. It became the basic structure of the further attempts we made in establishing our work. This symbiosis between the children with handicaps and the uprooted and homeless refugees had begun to show its results. Our special situation, combined with the ideas of Rudolf Steiner's science of the spirit, gave us the possibility to grow into a new social order.

This developing small commonwealth was like the dough; the morsel of the European destiny became the leaven and thus provided the substance of the Camphill movement. Its social order and its human structure was to become like a loaf of bread.

Three social endeavours

The forces which constitute the leaven of the bread of the social order of Camphill are threefold. They have their source in three historic attempts of community building, although these three endeavours failed outwardly, they none the less influenced very deeply the inner history of mankind during the last three centuries.

The three attempts have a single well from which they sprang. It was a little book, privately circulated from about 1610 onwards and, a few years later, also published and more widely read. The title of this pamphlet was *The Fama Fraternitatis of the Meritorious Order of the Rosy Cross, addressed to the Learned in General and the Governors of Europe.* It contained a short account of the Rosicrucian Brotherhood and an outline of the way in which a general brotherhood of people might come about. The pamphlet tried to prevent the incipient outbreak of the Thirty Years' War. It was a fruitless endeavour. The European nations were ready to fight and did it thoroughly. They achieved the destruction of a great part of Europe and a third of its population.

The *Fama Fraternitatis,* however, flowed like an underground stream through the minds and hearts of thousands of people and always made them try anew to attempt the impossible. Since this little pamphlet appeared there has been an almost continuous and uninterrupted flow of trials in community building first in Europe and later also in North America. Many futile attempts, many vain endeavours and several hideous efforts were made. The main ones were connected with three men:

  John Amos Comenius (1592–1670)
  Ludwig, Count Zinzendorf (1700–1760)
  Robert Owen (1771–1858)

In three consecutive centuries each one of them in his own way attempted a formation of a brotherhood of people. Comenius was a philosopher and an educator; Zinzendorf a Christian missionary, and Owen a social reformer. They handed on the cresset of their ideals from one to the other. Comenius had certainly read the *Fama Fraternitatis*. Zinzendorf knew of Comenius, as he received the ring of the bishopric of the Bohemian-Moravian Brotherhood of which Comenius was the last carrier. Owen knew of Zinzendorf and was, in his early youth, connected to the movement of religious revival which had one of his roots in Zinzendorf's work. Thus these three men, although they had never met (as the former had died before the next one was born), formed a continuous chain of the 'universal reformation' to which the *Fama Fraternitatis* referred. In their destiny the three show a gradual shift towards the west.

 John Comenius was born in the most eastern part of Central Europe, in the province of Moravia. His parents belonged to the original Bohemian Church. After studying theology and philosophy at various universities in Germany, he returned to his native country and, in 1616 was ordained as priest and deacon of the Unitas Fratrum. He remained in Moravia until 1628, but had to leave together with his congregation, as the repressive measures against non-Catholics became unbearable. He settled first in Poland and was, in 1632 consecrated as bishop of the Bohemian Brotherhood. As a result of the Thirty Years' War, Comenius, deprived of all his possessions, left Poland and visited England in 1641/42.[1]

John Amos Comenius (1592–1670), Nikolaus Ludwig Zinzendorf (1700–1760), Robert Owen (1771–1858). The pictures that illustrated the original publication were afterwards framed by König for his study in Camphill House (now a room of the Karl König Archive) as shown here.

Afterwards he went to Holland and Sweden and back to Poland. He was a refugee until in 1656 he found, at last, a home in Amsterdam. Influential friends provided the means for him and his family and he then had the possibility to publish a great number of books. Several times he had been driven away from the eastern provinces of Europe and found friends and a certain understanding for his work in Holland and England.

Ludwig Zinzendorf's family originally came from Austria. His grandfather had to leave his home as he was a Lutheran and did not want to submit to the powers of the Austrian Emperor, who demanded that all his people revert to Roman Catholicism. The family settled in Saxony where Zinzendorf was born. As young man he had been influenced by the Pietist movement which flourished in Germany at the beginning of the eighteenth century. This religious revival made the young man into the founder of a great brotherhood of which remnants still survive in various places all over the world. In Herrnhut, in Saxony, the first congregation was formed whose initial members were refugees from Bohemia, members of the Moravian

Brotherhood. Throughout the years, many more people joined the *Herrnhuter Brüdergemeine*. New settlements were founded all over Europe and several of the brethren went overseas on missionary work.

Zinzendorf visited England several times and was twice in North America where he inspected the newly founded congregations and preached in many places. He wandered from place to place, fought the many enemies inside and outside his brotherhood, inspired his friends and pupils and tried to overcome his own shortcomings and become a true Christian. He died in 1760 in Herrnhut and thousands of his brethren attended the funeral.

Robert Owen was the son of Welsh people. Already as a child he had shown outstanding intelligence; when not yet eight years old, he was the assistant of his teacher and taught a great number of pupils the three Rs. When he was ten years of age he left his family and became as apprentice at a draper's shop in Lincolnshire. A few years later he was in Manchester as the managing director of a huge mill with five thousand workers. In 1800, when not yet thirty years old, he was director and part-owner of a big mill in New Lanark near Glasgow. It was here that he started his great experiment in community building. For more than twenty years it remained a flourishing and shining example to humanity. From all over the world visitors came to see this miracle of a social experiment. Owen's intense idealism however, looked for more and greater things.

He started a new community in the state of Indiana in North America. After a short time (in 1825), the experiment failed entirely and Owen returned to England. From then onwards his life was an long and continuous battle; a struggle with the impeding forces of that age; a fight against complacency, against narrow-mindedness, against tyranny and the exploitation of the poor. He wrote innumerable books, papers and pamphlets and delivered many thousands of lectures all over Britain. He initiated the trade union movement. He created the first sick-fund for the workers and fought for the human rights of every adult and child.

He spent his last days in his native town of Newton in Wales, where he died on November 17, 1858.

What do these three men have in common? They all longed for a reformed human community. They imagined a new social order wherein a true brotherhood could be established. They strove for universal understanding among all people. According to their time, the three attempts were very different, yet they complemented each other.

Comenius

Comenius was a priest. His main interest, however, was philosophy and education. He was the founder of an entirely new educational system built on the combination of word and picture. His *Great Didactic* contains his teaching system which states:

> It is accordingly required of man that:
> 1. He should know all things
> 2. He should have power over all things and over himself.
> 3. He should refer himself and all to God, the source of all.

For, to Comenius, 'this life is only a preparation for an eternal life. The visible world is a seed-plot, a boarding house and training school for man.'[2] And 'nature gives the seeds of knowledge, virtue and morality but it does not give knowledge, virtue and religion themselves, these have to be striven for.'

Learning is a never-ending process. Therefore Comenius' great pansophic ideal was the formation of a Universal College which should become the fountain-head of all learning, an institution for the advancement of the whole of mankind. He once said about this idea:

> It is hardly necessary to describe how indispensable a School of Schools or Didactic College would be, in whatsoever part of the world it were founded ... the design itself should be cherished with a holy faith among the learned, pledged as they are, to promote God's glory in this very matter. These men should make it a subject of their combined labours to establish thoroughly the foundations of the sciences, to spread the light of wisdom throughout the human race with greater success than has heretofore been attained and to benefit mankind by new and useful inventions.[3]

Comenius imagined the future of man enlightened by the light of wisdom and learning, bringing everlasting peace and mutual understanding to all living people and creatures. Through wisdom only, man will be able to find his way to Christ and, through him, to God. This, to Comenius is the first and *Unum Necessarium*.

He never achieved the realisation of his great vision. In a rather distorted form it appeared as some of the learned societies in various parts of the world; one among them was and still is the Royal College. Comenius succeeded fully as an educationist. His *Orbis Pictus,* the first proper school-book ever written, remained for almost 200 years the standard book of learning for millions of children. Comenius is the teacher of modern Europe.

Zinzendorf

In Zinzendorf the impulse of the new social order remained mainly in the religious field. What for Comenius was learning, was for Zinzendorf faith. He once said, 'I herewith state that there is no Christianity without community.'[4] His work did not lie in writing learned books. During his lifetime he delivered about ten thousand sermons and addresses and he wrote about two thousand religious poems which were sung during the divine services of his great brotherhood.

He tried very hard to live in imitation of the life of Christ and the following words, taken from a letter to his wife, are typical of his attitude:

> The Saviour was at night on the mountains and during the day so occupied with work that often he never had time to eat or to sit down. If I have a very hard time and am overladen with work, I simply remember that he too, for our sake, had a very bitter life.

It is rather a childish attitude, but full of goodwill and great devotion. Zinzendorf was able to impart this quality to all his followers. Like the first Christians, they shared all things. They lived a simple life regulated by work and worship. They tried to be 'brethren in Christ'.

When, in 1727, the spiritual foundation of the first Brotherhood in Herrnhut was celebrated in the form of a common sacramental meal, Zinzendorf said:

> The whole of Herrnhut is founded on love and built through love and needs to be preserved by love. No difference may here exist, for devotion unites the hearts.

From this foundation onwards, the hourly prayers were introduced. At every hour throughout the day and night one of the brothers or sisters folded their hands and prayed to God. One is reminded of the never-ending choir which the Irish monks in the monastery of Bangor, performed. Throughout night and day their sacred songs reached up to heaven.

In the course of the following years, many more settlements of the new brotherhood were started and missionaries went out to North and South America, to Lapland and South Africa, to Ceylon and Ethiopia, to Malaya and Persia. The Moravian

Brotherhood began to preach the Gospel all over the world. It was a community of people built on the qualities of the human heart without adhering to any fundamentally new theology. It was the urge to give their lives and beings for the sake of Christ and his Apostles. Zinzendorf often asserted that he had no general plan or central idea which he pursued.

> Year after year I follow in the steps of my Saviour and do what I ought to do gladly ... I intend to visit as many heathens as possible and to see whether they will partake in the blood which was shed for the sake of the whole world.

Zinzendorf was, first and foremost, a preacher. He opened his heart and never spared its innermost substance. Not in thoughts, but in words he proclaimed a new brotherhood of men.

Owen

Robert Owen was an entirely different man. He was a bundle of will and energy and by no means as thinker. Very early, as a boy of fourteen, he had drawn up his fundamental ideas and, in his autobiography which he wrote as a very old man, he recollects it in the following way:

> It was with the greatest reluctance and after long contests in my mind, that I was compelled to abandon my first and deep-rooted impressions in favour of Christianity. But being obliged to give up my faith in this sect, I was at the same time compelled to reject all others, for I had discovered that all had been based on the same absurd imagination, that each man formed his own qualities – determined his own thoughts, will and action – and was responsible for them to God and to his fellowmen.

> My own reflections made me come to very different conclusions. My reason taught me that I could not have made one of my own qualities – that were forced upon me by Nature; that my language, religion and habits were forced upon me by Society; and that I was entirely the child of Nature and Society; that Nature gave the qualities and Society directed them. Thus I was forced, through seeing the error of their foundation to abandon all belief in every religion which had been taught to man. But my religious feelings were immediately replaced by the spirit of universal charity – not for a sect or party, or a country or a colour – but for the human race and with a real and ardent desire to do them good.[5]

In these sentences the whole of Owen's philosophy is contained. He was convinced that every human being is determined by his surroundings and that a change in the environment to the better, will radically change the qualities of men. A good environment will create honest people, a bad environment scoundrels and drunkards. Religion was to Owen an unnecessary appendix because he was convinced that in a community of good and moral men, no ills would ever arise.

Nevertheless, Owen himself was a deeply religious man as he believed with all his power in this 'spirit of universal charity,' for which he laboured all his life. He was the great protagonist against the evils of child labour in the industrial mills of his time. He proposed and developed amazing schemes to fight unemployment on great scale. To this end, he tried to establish big settlements for a few thousands of people, which were to be arranged in such a way that no individual would receive wages. Everything, work and pleasure, would be on a communal basis; common meals, common duties, common income, common benefits. He elaborated big schemes about the part each individual would play in this small, but self-regulated and self-contained communities.

He founded many such places but none of them really succeeded. Owen, however, was never down-hearted. He saw himself as the prophet of a new age and he expected the millennium to be imminent. When he started one of the many periodicals which he continually produced he wrote the following introduction:

> The Rubicon between he Old Immoral and the New Moral World is finally passed; and Truth, Knowledge, Union, Industry and Moral Good now take the field and openly advance against the united powers of Falsehood, Ignorance, Dis-union and Moral Evil ... the First Coming of the Christ was a partial development of Truth to the few, conveyed, of necessity, in dark sayings, parables and mysteries. The Second Coming of Christ will make Truth known to the many and enable to enjoy the endless benefits in practice, which it will assure to mankind. The time is, therefore, arrived when the foretold Millennium is about to commence, when the slave and the prisoner, the bondsman and the bondswoman, the child and the servant, shall be set free for ever and oppression of body and mind shall be known no more.

These are, no doubt, the words of man who regards himself as a prophet. This faith gave him an unbelievable amount of strength and vitality. He never faltered; he carried on undisturbed by the hundreds of disasters which befell him and the thousands of errors which he committed. He was like a giant who tried to change the whole trend of man's history and who led hundreds and thousands which he imagined in a rather illusionary picture. In spite of his mistakes and his wild fantasies, he inspired thousands and created social communities which will give guidance to the human commonwealth of the future.

The three ideals living in Camphill

These three men have spoken. Their words and deeds are still alive wherever a community of people strive to find their way towards a new social order. The words and deeds of the three are especially alive and active in the Camphill movement. Like the light of the three stars their beings radiate into our efforts and penetrate our work. But it is neither repetition of their sayings nor a conventional tradition we try to continue. We do not regard ourselves as pupils of Comenius or followers of Owen; nor are we members of the Moravian Brotherhood. But we feel that we walk in the trials and errors and achievements of these three great pioneers.

Since the last of the three, Robert Owen, died, a fourth appeared and took up their cresset in a new way. Rudolf Steiner was born in 1861, three years after the death of Owen. As a young man he was a philosopher; later, from the beginning of the twentieth century onwards, he renewed the understanding of Christ and Christianity. During the last years of his life he became a social reformer and showed new ways in many spheres of human activity; in medicine and education, in art and architecture. He enlivened these branches of human culture with the life of the spirit. He unified and enhanced all that which the three, independently of one another, had created.

In this way, the work of Comenius, Zinzendorf, and Owen finds a new breath of life in Rudolf Steiner's science of the spirit. What for Comenius three hundred years ago was his pansophia has appeared as Anthroposophia, the being of anthroposophy. The study of the spirit is an ever-renewing form of the Universal College which Comenius had envisaged. Whenever the books and lectures of Rudolf Steiner are studied by individuals and by groups of people, then a building stone for the Universal College is created.

Zinzendorf's deeds also need a renewal. He was a child of his time, which was penetrated by the Pietistic stream of faith and charity. There was an active longing for the *Imitatio Christi* and the dream of the imminence of the millennium permeated thousands of souls. Many felt to be the chosen people and pride and vanity entered their hearts. To recognise the Christ anew to believe in him as the light and strength of every attempt for the building of a community was made possible by Rudolf Steiner.

Robert Owen's active energy and drive worked in the dark. He was not able to illuminate it with the light of true knowledge and wisdom. He was a genius of practical social work. Not until Rudolf Steiner formulated the fundamental social law for the first time in 1906, could the innermost attempts of Owen be understood. This law is as follows:

> In a community of human beings working together, the well-being of the community will be the greater, the less the individual claims for himself the proceeds of the work he has himself done; that is, the more of these proceeds he makes over to his fellow workers, and the more his own requirements are satisfied not out of his own work done, but out of work done by the others.[6]

And Rudolf Steiner adds: 'Every community, indeed, would fall to pieces at once, if ... [it contradicts this law, and would bring] want and poverty and suffering in its train.' Here we meet Robert Owen's innermost aim. His life was a search for this law.

The Camphill movement attempts, wherever it labours and whatever work it does, to bring to realisation the ideals of these three men enlivened and furthered through anthroposophy.

By studying the whole field of anthroposophy in all its aspects, the Camphill movement helps to build the Universal College of Comenius' pansophia.

By attempting to lead a Christian life, in observing the Christian festivals as the divine regulation of the seasons and by recognising the spirit of Christ as the true light of every

Rudolf Steiner

human community, the Camphill movement strives to walk in Zinzendorf's universal *Imitatio Christi*.

By bringing about, every day anew, the reality of the fundamental social law, the Camphill movement tries to help in establishing Owen's 'universal charity'.

These three great pioneers are like the three wise men, who, once upon a time. laid their gifts at the feet of the Child during the first Christmas on earth. Comenius brought the gold of his wisdom. Zinzendorf offered the frankincense of his love. Owen gave the myrrh of his good will.

The Three Pillars of the Camphill Movement

The tasks of Camphill

Twenty-one years ago the seed of Camphill was sown. It grew and sprouted in several directions and gradually unfolded into the Camphill movement. This movement, being a living entity can hardly be defined in a few words. It has boundaries, but it is difficult to describe them. They exist as a reality for those who experience the essential being of the movement. Others may sense these boundaries; many believe, that such frontiers cannot be found.

The latter are the people who ask, 'How does one become a member of the Camphill movement?' and are astonished, when they hear, that no such membership exists. The Camphill movement is neither an association, nor a club. The movement has a council of a specific nature. It is a kind of temporary body which meets twice a year for one purpose only: to survey the position of the movement and to discuss its past and its future task. When these meetings are over, the members of the council return to their daily work and are no longer councillors of the movement; they are matrons, doctors, superintendents, farmers, joiners, and so on.

Thus the movement remains fluid, alive and progressive. It is more an impulse than an idea. The impulse, however, tries to act in accordance with certain ideas. The movement and all who work in it, strive for these ideas with enthusiasm and fervour.

The movement is, therefore more than the sum total of the schools, homes, training centres, and so forth which are attached to it. There are also many individuals who work in the spirit of the movement and who feel united with it. Their efforts may later lead to the foundation of a school, a home, an agricultural holding, a curative centre, which by their nature will be part of the impulse.

The Camphill movement is no trade-mark. Anyone can call himself a part of it; the council of the movement may have to consider whether such an assertion is right or wrong. No court procedure need ever be called, because the movement is in itself strong enough to deny or assert whether a person or a group of people or a working community is affiliated to it or not.

The Camphill movement is not an economic entity. The various centres which are part of the movement are financially independent units. They are sometimes called upon to make contributions towards journeys undertaken for the furtherance of the Camphill impulse, towards letters written to keep the movement in touch with its centres or towards individual expenses incurred in the service of the whole movement. In this way, we were able to finance the beginning in Downington, Pennsylvania and certain other journeys which were made in the interest of the work. In a similar way some of the centres make contributions to keep our London centre going.

The Camphill movement has so far had one main task: curative education. It would, however, be wrong to think that this is the only aim of our work. It is the field of education and training of children with handicaps that has occupied us most. Since the Camphill Village Trust and the village community in Yorkshire was founded, another branch has grown from the main stem of the movement: the establishment of village communities for young men and women with handicaps.

There are, however, other aims ahead of us. One of the foremost tasks will be the care of the land. Gardens and farms today are ruined and exploited by mechanised work and chemical fertilisers. The soil all over the world is like someone who suffers and cries out for help and healing. It is to be hoped that the movement will find the right helpers to create remedial work in this field, too.

Other tasks are still hidden in the lap of the future. They will gradually call upon us to fulfil their demands. The Camphill movement is young enough to expect many years of work to come. I can foresee tasks in many fields of human endeavour: in education and medicine, in agriculture and industry, art and music. Our hopes should not reach too high, but they should not confine themselves to fields that are too narrow.

What we must keep in mind are the three fundamental ideals of which we have already spoken: the stars of Comenius, Zinzendorf and Owen. To bring these ideals to a realisation will always have to be our aim.

Comenius' ideals in the college meeting

The first star is the Universal College of which Amos Comenius dreamed three hundred years ago. The pansophia he imagined was re-created in Anthroposophia, the being of anthroposophy. This is borne out by some remarks Rudolf Steiner once made. Speaking about Comenius he said:

> We can see how a beginning was made in the sixteenth and seventeenth centuries of what we can now take up and further in our own efforts for humanity's evolution. Then what we seek will be very much the right thing ... what the evolution of humanity requires and necessitates.[1]

John Amos Comenius (1592–1670)

Rudolf Steiner pointed out, how in Comenius a certain insight arose which is further developed in the teaching of anthroposophy. Comenius was a teacher; the same can be said of Rudolf Steiner. He also brought a new approach to the education of the child, the normal as well as those with handicaps. Like Comenius, Rudolf Steiner did not stop at the education of children. He attempted far more. Anthroposophical Societies were founded to become a platform for the furtherance of spiritual science. The groups and societies were meant to help the spreading and ever wider propagation of anthroposophy.

The Camphill movement will never intend to be an anthroposophical group or society. It is not the task of the movement to spread science of the spirit, but it is its task to be permeated by anthroposophy. We continually endeavour to establish spiritual science in our work so that the fruits of our labour bear witness to the truth of anthroposophy. In this way, many of those who join us to learn and experience Curative Education meet anthroposophy. Our, friends, the parents of the children who are sent to us, visitors and helpers encounter the name and ideas of Rudolf Steiner, often for the first time. Nevertheless, it is not our task to propagate his teachings; our endeavours are to help and to heal. We know that we can do so when we teach, treat, educate and carry out our work in the light of his indications.

We must learn to find the appropriate way of studying anthroposophy I do not mean the individual study by reading books and lectures; this is the task of each person who aims to acquaint himself ever more with the science of the spirit. The task of the movement is to attempt a common experience of anthroposophy in such a form that it becomes an ever renewed spiritual event.

For many years we have experienced the great importance of our college meetings. Every week the staff of a house or a whole estate meet in order to discuss one of the children under their care. The child's case-history is read and then the teachers, helpers and nurses give their report and impressions of the child in question. Many symptoms, signs and features are collected until – usually under the guidance of one of the doctors – the image of the child arises. His habits, achievements, faults and failures are laid out in such a way that gradually a complete picture of his individuality appears. The fundamental indications that Rudolf Steiner gave about the human being are the compass we follow. If such a college meeting succeeds, it is the result of a common effort of everyone who takes part of it. It then turns into a true symposium. To recognise the child's individual nature then leads to an awareness of the necessary curative and educational treatment.

The college meeting is the wellspring of our curative

educational work. The whole community of coworkers participates in it and achieves in a common spiritual effort the fundamental approach for each individual child. We may call this effort the 'pansophical' form of gaining true insight into the nature of an other human being. It is not a play with scientific terms, not a superficially laid-out puzzle of complexes, instincts and emotions, but an attempt to re-create in our mind the true nature of a personality.

To hold a college meeting is an art which has to be learned and it takes many years to become a master in this field. A great deal of individual study must be accomplished and a fair amount of knowledge of anthroposophy, medicine and psychology are necessary to conduct such a meeting to its final goal. If it succeeds, all who took part have made a new step in knowledge. Equally important, however, is the benefit derived by the child who was discussed. We have sometimes experienced that already on the next morning the child was fundamentally changed in his being and behaviour. He subconsciously experienced the great effort which was made to understand his special situation and responded quickly.

The weekly college meetings are the central expression of the movement's striving for anthroposophy. From this centre, many other attempts of 'pansophic' learning spring. These are the study groups of people within a common field of work. Teachers, doctors, nurses form these special study circles. There are several such groups in each of our centres. Here in Camphill [in Aberdeen], for instance, the curative teachers for deaf and blind children meet and discuss the fundamentals of their work. A teacher's college has regular meetings, a doctor's group assembles weekly and studies certain aspects of the work. In this way, a living adult education college has come about.

Besides such special groups, we must mention the various classes of the training course. In most of the centres of the Camphill movement this training course has been established. The students have lectures, lecture-demonstrations and classes in many subjects related to curative education. The training course is a branch of the college meeting. This training course, however, can sometimes also take the form of a conference when for a few days special theme is discussed in common. Our summer conference in 1959 on the problem of contact was such a short and comprehensive training course for the workers in the Camphill movement.

College meetings need not to be held on children only; a garden, a farm, a special question of the work, a problem of the present time, difficulties in the house, an epidemic – any such theme can become the content of a college meeting. It is quite unnecessary that discontent, despondency or even misery exist among the coworkers. A common symposium in the form of a college meeting can often help to overcome a difficult situation.

Comenius wrote in his *Temple of Pansophia:*

> The Solomonic Temple was built of stones which were hewn to perfection. During the erection of the temple no noise of any hammer, axe or iron tool was heard. Similarly when the Temple of Wisdom is built, neither quarrel nor discord shall exist; everything shall be working in a square so that it need only be put together.[2]

This is the pansophic ideal of Comenius. It appears again, permeated by anthroposophy, in the college meetings and all related functions, groups and bodies of the Camphill movement.

Zinzendorf's religious endeavour and the Bible Evening

The second star above the Camphill movement is Zinzendorf's attempt to form a Christian social order. It was his conviction that 'there is no Christianity without community.'[3] We would rather reverse this saying as we have experienced that there is no community without Christianity. Zinzendorf was the founder of a special chapel within the Protestant Church. He sometimes imagined that his *Brüdergemeine* would grow to such an extent that it would embrace all existing churches. A great deal of enthusiasm lived in him and in his early followers. Their hearts were filled with the same light that permeated the first followers of the apostles.

Nikolaus Ludwig Zinzendorf (1700–1760)

The Camphill movement, however, has no intention or desire to develop into a sect. It should therefore not be regarded as a sectarian community. It is far from it. For the Camphill movement, Christianity is an indispensable part of its life and work; it works *out of* Christianity, not *for* Christianity. Thus it is not an organisation for the purpose of disseminating Christian faith.

Just as the movement is not an anthroposophical group or society it is equally not a Christian sect or congregation. Those who work in and for the movement are entirely free to be members of any Christian church (or none), as well as of any group or society it they wish. It is a personal matter to belong to a church, a club, a society or an association. The Camphill movement is none of these; it is an attempt, an impulse, a community of men and women who try to live and work in common for a spiritual purpose.

The central event in our sphere of Christian existence is the Bible Evening. It corresponds to the college meeting in the realm of our pansophic ideal. Every Saturday in the evening, each house-community wherever and whatever its work may be, meets in order to prepare for the Sunday. The members of the house-community gather around the table, have a simple meal, speak of the events of the past week and then turn to that part of the gospel which will be read from he altar on Sunday. All are meant to prepare themselves through the week for this Bible Evening, because whoever is able to, should share with their friends the experiences they had when reading and thinking about the particular passage from the gospel.

These weekly gatherings create a strong and intimate bond among the coworkers. They meet in a sublime realm as brothers and sisters. None of them has any distinction other than his devotion to Christ and to his fellow human beings who sit with him around the same table for the same purpose. Thus the Bible Evening unites each house-community every week anew and whatever difficulties have arisen among the members of a house-community they now sit together at the table and turn their souls again towards a common aim. They meet each other anew in the true light of the spirit.

It is of great importance that throughout the movement everyone turns to the gospel daily. This presents a united inner task which creates strength and sense of purpose. That so many of us try to formulate our thoughts on the weekly passage of the gospel in order to speak about in the Bible Evening is an exercise in concentration and courage.

Through these efforts, the Sunday Services for the children and adolescents are properly prepared. The texts of these services were given to the religion teachers of the first Waldorf School by Rudolf Steiner and have since that time been used in many of the Steiner Schools for both normal children and those with handicaps. These services have become an integral part of our movement. We have learned to see the deep and lasting healing-power which they create in the children. Their souls are thirsty for the true religious draught and they drink it in every Sunday with the greatest devotion. Every child, however disturbed and disabled can follow the content of the service with its heart. The preparation of the teachers and helpers through the Bible Evening provides an added strength to this act of Christian worship.

In the Bible Evening as well as in the Sunday Services, children and adults approach the central event of the earth existence: the Mystery of Golgotha. This is the name which Rudolf Steiner coined for the deeds of Christ and which conveys their innermost meaning.

With the Bible Evening on Saturn-Day evening we open the door and then lead the children through it to the inner chapel on the Sun-Day on the following morning. Their meeting with the ever-present power of Christ – his light and his love – renew their strength as well as ours. We all partake in an act of reality and not one of remembrance; because we not only remember the deeds and the being of the Christ, but we partake in and suffer with his eternal presence. His words, 'I am with you always, even unto the end of the world,'[4] is a growing experience for many of us.

Just as the college meeting has branched out into groups and study-circles, so have Bible Evening and Sunday Services extended their substance and power into other activities: the regular morning and evening prayers with the children, the grace before each meal, the songs on Sunday morning and other similar observances.

There are especially the preparations for the festivals of the seasons and the great amount of care which is given to their arrangements. The children are led through Advent to Christmas and through Lent to Easter. For weeks, they hear the appropriate stories, legends and fairy-tales; they paint and model related subjects, filling the mind and heart with the meaning of each festival.

Special plays are prepared and rehearsed by the coworkers for Michaelmas, Christmas, Easter and St John's Day and the performances are shared by children, adolescents and adults. The plays lend a special character to each of the festivals and root them deeply into the individual soul. The festival plays, therefore, are not so much artistic performances as acts of faith. They can be likened to the mystery plays which were enacted in the churches during the Middle Ages. They are part of a sphere of which the Bible Evening is the centre.

This sphere, however, is permeated by the new revelations which Rudolf Steiner gave on the Mystery of Golgotha. He created a new understanding for the deeds of Christ. He made us comprehend the words of the gospels in a fresh light, and interpreted their meaning, so that the modern mind is able to follow. Rudolf Steiner did not only transform the pansophic ideal of Comenius into anthroposophy, he also permeated Zinzendorf's fervent *Imitatio Christi* into a new recognition of Christ. We adhere to his words:

> If you accept the spirit of Anthroposohia in reality, then you will find that it opens up he human ear, the human heart and the whole soul of man for the Mystery of

Christ. The whole destiny of Anthroposophia intends to be the destiny of Christianity.[5]

Owen's economic ideals and the fundamental social law

The third star which shines above Camphill and its Movement is Robert Owen's attempt towards a new economic order. It was his intention to re-create human society by reshaping its economic conditions. He was convinced that man is deeply influenced by his environment and that an appropriate surrounding will also create better people. He was in a sense a forerunner of a socialistic society and imagined that an even distribution of all material commodities would give an equal share of happiness to every person.

Robert Owen (1771–1858)

Robert Owen envisaged common ownership in the village-communities of which he dreamed. He imagined his villages with large community-houses and dining-rooms for about one or two thousand people, a recreation-hall for the same number and other big houses in which each family should occupy a room for themselves. The children would be educated apart from their parents, big creches and boarding-schools should care for them according to age. In this way – so Robert Owen thought – the children would develop into exemplary members of a directed and planned society.

The idea never materialised because already during the first years of establishing these attempted communities, they began to break down. This was mostly on account of human difficulties and only sometimes through lack of funds. Owen succeeded at one time: in his first settlement in New Lanark where he himself was able to direct the venture. The shining example of his personal life and conduct made this success possible. His strong personality inspired the men and women who worked in his mill.

Rudolf Steiner says of this attempt:

> He started, in New Lanark, model industries, in which
> he managed to employ the workers in such a way
> that they not only enjoyed a decent human existence
> in material respects, but also lived their lives under
> conditions that satisfied the moral sense.

New Lanark was small enough to be a successful experiment. All the bigger social ventures that Owen planned disintegrated. Rudolf Steiner sums up the conclusion to which Owen came in the following words:

> He was forced to the conviction that any good institution
> is only so far maintainable as the human beings
> concerned are disposed by their own inner nature to its
> maintenance and are themselves warmly attached to it.[6]

This points to the fundamental condition of an appropriate social order. The whole modern attempt in human relations is based on these simple facts. The very successful movement of Moral Re-Armament is nothing but a persevering attempt of human relations. Rudolf Steiner explained that whatever industrial or other institutions there may be, they can only be kept in a working and living order when those who work in them are inwardly connected with the work and its tools. This, however, is a question of responsibility.

If people handle only a lever in the course of a serial production-process, they will soon loose interest in their work. Their main concern will become the number of working hours and the wage packet at the end of the week. Production, but not the one who produces, can be socialised. As soon people have been given responsibility for the work they do, they have the possibility of identifying themselves with their labour. They will then be satisfied, even proud and happy with their achievements. Modern industrialists have begun to realise this fundamental law. Industrial psychologists and social workers are continually faced with the problems arising from this human need. On the other hand, the planned arrangements of modern industrial organisations tend to overlook the human factor.

In the Camphill movement due regard is paid to this fundamental principle. It must be our constant aim to help every coworker to become a responsible person, so that he shares the responsibility for the whole. It would be wrong to say that we work without any salary; it is superficial if not ill-disposed to make such a statement. None of us receives a wage packet at the end of the week or a cheque at the end of the month. Instead of being paid a salary, we learn to arrange the income and expenditure of the unit in which we work according to our own discretion. Each house, each workshop, each working-centre is an independent economic unit which is responsible for its own finances.

In this way, the Camphill movement has overcome the necessity of employing people. None of us is an employer or an employee. None of us regard the money which goes through our hands as personal possession. We do not earn money; we administer it. This we try to perform in the best way possible, but each does it according to his own responsibility and insight. We have appointed councils which control our management and give us advice and help.

Our work in whichever sphere we do it is done without the expectation to be paid; but we do expect to live under conditions which are appropriate to our personal needs. Thus we try to arrange our lives in accordance with the fundamental social law which Rudolf Steiner formulated:

> In a community of human beings working together, the well-being of the community will be the greater, the less the individual claims for himself the proceeds of the work he has himself done.[7]

That it is possible to work under such conditions and to share our efforts with our neighbours and not claim profit for ourselves is due to the establishment of the Bible Evening and the college meeting. These two institutions permeate our lives with a higher aim so that we work to fulfil our ideals. Here again, a fundamental indication of Rudolf Steiner gives us guidance and direction. He says that if someone works for another, he must find in the other the purpose for his own labours; and if someone has to work for a whole community, he has to sense and to experience the value, the being and the meaning of it. This is only possible if the community is something other than a more or less undefined sum of single people. Such a community must be permeated by a true spirit in which anyone of its members partakes. In such a community every person should say, 'This community is right and I want it to be so.' The community must have a spiritual mission and every individual should have the urge to help so that the mission may be fulfilled.

In former times, a nation or smaller social communities such as municipalities or counties were filled with a common task. The building of a temple or a cathedral, warfare, conquest or pilgrimage were such communal deeds. Conditions have fundamentally changed, and today it is only possible for such common tasks or missions to begin to live again in spiritual communities.

Basically, however, it is necessary that every member of a working community is kept fully informed of everything which belongs to the economic field and structure of his environment. Only if this is done will a coworker be able to develop a sense of responsibility for his work because he will see it as part of a greater totality. He can then participate in the spirit of the whole community. A school, a farm, factory, a hospital – in fact any place where people work together, can become such a totality. But they will never work in a human way, if every participant is eager to cash his own portion. It is never the question of sharing the cake in the most equal fashion. We can only share the work, not the proceeds. The latter can never be evenly distributed; as soon as this is done, injustice sets in, because every person has his own individual wants and if the one needs more, he other will require less.

As long as the work is shared according to the individual abilities of everyone, the needs and commodities of life will be available. Even stragglers can be accommodated if the crew is willing to carry them along. Not to work can sometimes be as important as to work. This should, however, not turn into a habit, but be a time of inner recovery or self-recognition.

When we more and more learn to manage this form of economic life, the movement will plant a seed for a new social order. In the same way that money will never be our personal property, also our houses, grounds or equipment are not personal possessions. They do not even belong to the movement, but are, like the money, administered by it. The single individual may possess whatever he may wish. He might still feel the need to own furniture, books, capital; in so far as he is an individual he may be in need of earthly goods. As a worker in the movement, he is without property, without any income and equal to those who work with him.

In this way, we will achieve some of the conditions for which Robert Owen strove. He did not succeed because he tried to share the proceeds and the profit of the work which was done. We work for the sake of work; we do not expect a return because we gradually learn to understand that the returns are a gift, a donation, an act of good will which the others provide for us. We give and thereby receive. Thus the innermost secret of all labour begins to reveal itself: it is love and nothing but unending love. It is the love and charity of which St Paul speaks in the First Letters to the Corinthians.

Liberty, equality and fraternity

The college meeting, the Bible Evening and the attempt to realise the fundamental social law in the economic field as it was formulated by Rudolf Steiner are the three pillars of the Camphill movement. Wherever working groups and centres of the movement are established, there the three pillars will have to be erected in order to carry the framework in which our work can proceed.

The single centres are not meant to copy one another in their attempts to build the three pillars; they need to be adapted to the individual structure of each of these centres. In Holland or in South Africa the part which the Bible Evening or the college meeting plays will be somewhat different from the form and arrangements assumed in Camphill in Scotland. No rigid dogma can be applied; the fluctuating variability of the individual needs of life in each of the houses and establishments must be recognised.

This asks for special attention in those places where curative education is not the main part of the work. In the Botton Village Community no college meeting can be held, for it would injure the dignity of the young villagers if they were to be discussed by their friends and helpers. Another social form which replaces the college meeting will have to be found. Equally the Bible Evening has to undergo a metamorphosis as the Sunday Service differs from those held in Camphill. In spite of such changes, the essence of both institutions (Bible Evening and college meeting) remains an integral part of the social life of the Village.

Fundamental changes come about in the economic sphere when places like the Village begin to produce goods and articles for sale on the open market. As soon as this happens (as it has already begun to happen in Botton Village), the various production centre such as the weaving shop, the joinery workshop, the soft toy and dollmaking workshop – need to co-operate and form an association. They should become financially independent of one another but at the same time, share a considerable part of the capital they have earned to help one another to compete on the open market. No money should ever be stored, but always ploughed back into the needs of the establishments and the commodities of the coworkers.

Should the time come, when purely agricultural centres will be units of the Camphill movement, other variations will be necessary. The college meetings will then concern themselves with fields and gardens, with the livestock and the farm as a living entity. The Bible Evenings will be necessary for the whole farm community, and the basic social law will assume an especially important function.

In this way the three pillars on which the movement is built, will always have to be regarded as the fundamental structure of our work. With this in mind, we must ask after the deeper significance of the three principles. Are we already able to describe their meaning? If we liken the movement to a growing child, its development will depend on three basic qualities:

the ability to walk, to speak and to think. The mind and the being of the child would never properly unfold, if these three gifts bestowed on man, would not develop. The human body develops its uprightness when the ability to walk is acquired. The human soul unfolds it innermost quality when it learns to speak the mother-tongue. The human spirit begins to shine when it attempts to make the first tentative steps in thinking. What these three qualities are for the child, the three pillars are for the Camphill movement.

The basic social law gives the movement is uprightness. It does not run or jump or climb with vehemence and zeal and fitness as do other economic enterprises. The basic social law enables the various centres of the movement to become master of their economic conditions. Money is there to help and not to hinder; it is meant to be a servant and not a tyrant. The basic social law bestows human dignity on a working community of people. Such a community can stand upright and govern its economic conditions with clarity. It will never have any financial successes, but it will maintain a sound and orderly economy which will enable it to cover all needs and necessities.

The Bible Evening fills the movement with a common language. Not only can the coworkers understand one another when they sit around the table on Saturday evening; they learn to have regard for one another and to acquire a human attitude to all their fellow men and the work they do. This common language permeates our souls and make each one of us gradually become a disciple of Christianity. The language of the Bible Evening is a deeply unifying force throughout the movement.

The college meeting and all other efforts related to it give us the freedom of thought which only anthroposophy can confer to people of today. This is not a unifying but an individualising power. In the college meeting each single person is like the instrument in an orchestra. It plays its own melody or harmony, but makes the whole symphony resound. The college meeting enables us to acquire the living forces of thinking; we strive to gain the new image of man in the way Rudolf Steiner revealed it to our age.

The movement is like a human being, who learns to walk, to speak and to think under the guidance of Comenius, Zinzendorf and Robert Owen. They are the three wise men who bestow their gifts to the child.

Once, the French Revolution intended to establish the three great ideals of our modern age: liberty, equality and fraternity. The evil powers of French nationalism destroyed these three ideals and turned them into their opposite. Rudolf Steiner revived them again when he proclaimed the idea of the threefold social order. He described how liberty must rule in the sphere of the free spiritual life, how equality has its justification in the realm of rights, and that fraternity is the only possible relation among men in the sphere of the economic order.

Thus in the movement, we become brothers in the economic field, we are all equal around the table of the Bible Evening and we acquire our freedom in the sphere of the college meeting. We share our work in brotherhood, we are equal before the face of Christ, we are free as individuals when we acquire anthroposophy. In this way we try to become true human beings so that we can serve mankind.

The Three Essentials of Camphill

Looking back to the early beginnings twenty-five years ago, we can observe a slow uphill advance. It is by no means a story of success and splendour. It is a tale of trial and error, of hard labour and of many failures.

Twenty-five years is a long time! Much greater things have happened in the course of quarter of a century. But Camphill had to grow against many odds and – to begin with – under rather unfavourable conditions. It has, nevertheless, made its way and will continue to pursue its aims. The goal is still far ahead.

Materially we began with next to nothing. Around us was a foreign country and almost the whole world at war. We – a small band of refugees – were classified as 'enemy aliens' and most of us had to spend many months in an internment camp. After our release the war gathered strength and fury and the country was fully occupied combatting a deadly onslaught.

During this turmoil of 'blood, toil, tears and sweat' the seed of Camphill slowly began to sprout. The silent message of the child with handicaps reached a number of parents, doctors, and teachers. Education authorities heard of our effort and sent some of their charges to Camphill. An increasing number of inquiries reached our office and the available space was soon unable to satisfy the demand.

We, therefore, tried to acquire or rent some neighbouring estates in order to enlarge our work. A few helpers and friends joined the original nucleus of people, but not nearly enough to carry the spreading task satisfactorily. There were far too many children for the handful of coworkers. Only by sheer grace, and the greatest sacrifice on the part of everyone, could this difficult period be surmounted. But gradually relief and help came.

The war changed into peace; frontiers were opened and young people came from the Continent to help us. More and more parents, relieved from the heavy burden of the war, supported our efforts, and some influential people gave us advice and counsel. The seed of Camphill had already grown into a small plant. Branches developed and attempted to sprout through their own strength.

And one day, a few buds began to appear on one or other twig of this tiny bush. They unfolded into flowers and radiated their beauty and scent into our hearts. These flowers were the inner victories of our external labour and work: the improvement we observed in some of the children, the peace slowly achieved in daily life, the silent wonder during the services on Sunday morning, the sudden understanding of the innermost nature of one or another of the children – these were the things that made our work worthwhile.

We gradually became aware of the beauty of these flowers. We began to realise that their radiance gave us strength and perseverance. But there were long stretches of time when the bush of Camphill had no flowers. The leaves of everyday life just continued to grow, but no further fresh buds appeared. Then suddenly and unexpectedly, a whole branch burst out again into blossom; and it even occurred a few times that all over the movement a sea of flowers unfolded in wondrous beauty. These were the times when the ideals of Camphill were strong enough to permeate our life and work. For these flowers are the essentials of Camphill which appear, shine forth and wither away again. Some of the flowers, however, are fertilised and change into fruits. When this occurs, we can clearly observe the results of our labour. With each fruit we make another step in the understanding of our children, of our work and our task. These fruits will never perish. They remain, endure and feed our further efforts.

The essentials of Camphill are these fruits and flowers; when they fail to unfold and grow, Camphill will not be able to develop and to keep its pledge to the handicapped child.

Recognising the spirit in each human being

Many times the question is asked; what is the difference between Camphill and other residential schools and homes which care so efficiently for children with handicaps? [The answer is by no means easy nor simple. Twenty years ago this difference was obvious. Other homes – with few exceptions – made no attempt to help children with handicaps in their development. The children were properly cared for but were just kept in a kind of benevolent custody.][1]

[This has changed fundamentally.] Today the whole civilised world is aware that even severe mental handicap can be improved under remedial education. [In this respect Camphill was once a voice in the wilderness. Today this is no longer the case. The voice was heard and thousands came to be baptised for the sake of the handicapped child.] In schools, homes and hospitals remedial education, occupational therapy and therapeutic communities are already a general rule.

The children with handicaps are no longer looked upon as imbeciles and a burden to the community. Their human abilities are recognised and great efforts are being made to treat and train, to teach and help these children.

To us, as pupils of Rudolf Steiner, the child – whatever his mental condition may be – is more than his physical appearance may indicate. He is more than his body, more than his emotions, more than his spoken or unspoken words. He is even more than his achievements. In his appearance he is merely the outer shell of an infinite and eternal spiritual being.

What does this mean? We are convinced that every human being has his individual existence not only here on earth between birth and death, but that every child was a spiritual entity before he was born, and that every human being will continue to live after he has passed through the gate of death. Thus, any kind of physical or mental handicap is not acquired by chance or misfortune. It has a definite meaning for the individual and is meant to change his life.

Like any other human being who has to battle with various diseases, the child with handicaps also has to learn how to live with his ailment or to conquer it. As parents and teachers, our task is to appeal to the eternal being of the child, to make him recognise his destiny. However hidden his individuality may be and however covered up by the many layers of inability, lameness and uncontrolled emotions – we must try to break through these sheaths and reach the holy of holies in every human being: the seat of his spiritual entity.

The conviction that everyone carries this 'I' in him and that this 'I' is eternal, imperishable and of a spiritual nature, is fundamental for our approach to the child. He is our brother and our sister. He is equal to every other human being and equal to us. We do not deal with the handicapped child; we deal with the child who is handicapped.

Many of them are retarded, paralysed, epileptic, incompetent, lazy, abnormal or backward. All this may be as it appears. The nucleus of the being, the inmost kernel of his existence is not only infinite; it is divine! It is part of the divinity to which it will return and from whence it came and will come again. His crippled and distorted life is but one among many such lives on his way back to the Father. We are all prodigal sons seeking our ways back to the house of the eternal ground of the world, the fountainhead of our existence. This is the first essential of Camphill.

Self-development

And the second? Three times the gospels relate the story of the young man who suffered from epilepsy and whom the disciples could not heal. Only Christ – after having gone through the stage of Transfiguration – was able to cast out the evil spirit. And when the disciples asked him why they themselves were helpless, he replied, 'Because of your little faith. For truly, I say to you, if you have faith as a grain of mustard seed, you will say to this mountain, "Move from here to there," and it will move; and nothing will be impossible to you' (Matt.17:20).

This saying should not be taken literally but spiritually. It simply indicates that man is endowed with a power which has creative possibilities. This power can build houses and temples; it paints pictures and forms sculptures; it is the same power which invented the wheel, spanned the first bridges over a river and trained horses. This is the power which can move mountains and has done so throughout mankind's evolution.

This inner force is not man's intellect nor his intelligence. It is his ability to transform nature. It is the creative force which changes wild sceneries into lovely landscapes; the force which tills the soil and invented the potter's wheel and the weaver's loom.

This creative power is gradually fading away. Our technical civilisation no longer has any place for it. The gadgets and machines do all the 'creative work' which every human being was called upon to do until the beginning of the twentieth century. This transformation is quite justified in the sphere of industrial production and everyday life. It is right to substitute central heating for an open fireplace and a washing machine for a wooden tub. It is already questionable whether a horse-drawn plough can be replaced by a tractor. And where a human being is concerned there should be no question whether machines can replace the creative ability of man. No teaching machine can be substituted for the teacher; no mechanical means for the direct contact between one human being and another.

The 'grain of mustard seed' of creativity is one of the fundamentals in remedial education. It has to be renewed day after day in those who work with child with handicaps. This faith 'to be able to move mountains' is the prerogative of the teacher and helper in the field of mental deficiency. He must acquire it, otherwise his work becomes stale.

Rudolf Steiner drew attention to this need in his lectures on curative education. He said, 'In educating handicapped children ... we are making ... a deep intervention in karma. Whenever we give treatment to a handicapped child, we are intervening in karma.'[2] We, as teachers and doctors, can only do the work for these children if we engender in our souls the creative power which may be able to remove or at least lower the mountain of handicap.

To kindle this inner power should be the daily exercise of the teacher. He has to educate himself and to gain a steady certainty in his responsibility and conscientiousness: his responsibility for the destiny of the child; his conscientiousness for the work with his child – these are the two indispensable virtues of the curative teacher.

If the teacher and helper can achieve this, then spiritual sources are opened up and intuition will guide and replenish his labour. Every morning and evening the teacher must turn to this fountainhead of his existence; be it in prayer and meditation, or concentration or other mental exercises. Such inner education has to be pursued. Otherwise the teacher's strength will fail and his most precious gift, spiritual courage, will vanish.

As curative teachers we need undaunted energy and courage. Nothing but prayer and meditation can create this special faculty in the human soul of today. And when the disciples asked further why they were unable to cast out the evil spirit from the boy, Christ answered: 'This kind cannot be drive forth by anything but prayer and fasting' (Matt.17:21).

Again – such words of Christ cannot be taken literally. We neither cast out spirits nor do we need to fast. 'To cast out spirits' means to create a surrounding congenial to a child with handicaps. It is an environment of loving peace and peaceful love. It is a house without noise and hurry, without restlessness and quarrel. And 'to fast' means to forego the various temptations today's life offers us: television, radio, drink, chatter, gossip and the many things that make life so difficult and unbearable. This type of everyday existence is the greatest enemy of these children.

If we are able to renounce these temptations and lead a life without that glamour, we do justice to the child with handicaps by 'praying and fasting'.

Who will understand this? Today millions of cripples, disabled and impaired people are 'entertained' all over the world by the powers of wireless and television. With the best of intentions the worst influence is thus brought to bear. None of our houses in Camphill has television; and the radio is only turned on when special occasions make it necessary.

The inner education of the teacher is the second essential of Camphill. His endurance and sacrifice, his continued care of the child and his attempt 'to fast and pray', thereby creating 'the grain of mustard seed' in his soul, is this second essential. We try to prepare it during our training courses. Not only knowledge is given to our students. They learn to kindle their creative forces and to make them into a continuous source of strength and sacrifice.

Establishing a community

The third essential is the following: During the last two decades a new science has markedly moved into the foreground of common knowledge: sociology. Though it is an old science it had never been in the consciousness of the general public. But today everybody speaks about human relations, interpersonal relationships, social psychology, etc. This is due to the growing awareness that every human being is largely dependent on his environment and under the deep and direct influence of his fellow human beings.

We have learned to understand the lasting influence which a

mother has on her baby. We know that no infant will grow up unharmed without the loving care and personal dependence he receives from his environment. We have begun to recognise an astounding way the character of an individual is determined by the family. We have become conscious of the influence that a larger community exerts on each of its members.

In fact, we have become convinced through an overwhelming number of observations that the human being is – to use a word from Aristotle – a *zoön politikon,* a social creature. *(Zoön* for the Greeks was a 'living being' and not an 'animal' in today's sense and meaning.) Man is a social being! We might almost say: the human being can only then be a human being when he is part of a human community. An isolated person is unable to develop his humanness. Everyone is dependent on others, and not only has to communicate with others but also and be recognised by the other. Every 'I' needs its 'you', every 'my' its 'your'. This is true for every human being, for the healthy as well as one who is ill, for the bright person as well as for one who is slow. Community – in whatever form – is the essential matrix of the human being.

This social womb has several layers. The innermost one is the family, the second is represented by the village or the street and district of the town. The third layer is the community of the people who speak the same language. And the outermost and largest layer is the whole of mankind. Just as no embryo can live outside the layers of the womb, the human being who has been born cannot live outside the womb of human community. We are born out of one womb into the other; from out of our mother's womb into the womb of society. And every newborn must learn to adjust from the one environment to the other. If there is not enough loving guidance and gentle care, this adjustment will be difficult and sometimes even impossible.

Many children with disabilities suffer severely from this maladjustment in early childhood. The disappointment of the parents, the misunderstanding of the environment, the inability to understand their strange appearance and unusual behaviour drives them into isolation. This happens far more often than we realise. For this reason, creating a suitable social surrounding with the appropriate layers of community living for disabled children and young adults is one of the most important requirements for every kind of remedial education. This is the real basis for work with cognitively, developmentally impaired individuals. Since the beginnings of Camphill, we were conscious of this basic need in our work. And we have never ceased to readjust our social structure and remodel it according to changing conditions.

Superficial observers and brief visitors often judge our way of life with a preconceived opinion. The fact that none of our coworkers receives a wage or salary is not an economic arrangement but part of our social endeavour to create the right environment for the person with handicaps. We are convinced that we could not do our work in the right way if we were employees and received a salary, because we know that work which is paid for has lost its social value. No professional person can be paid for his services. As soon that happens it is no longer a service. It is remuneration, not money, that creates a barrier between the one who gives and the one who receives. Giving and receiving is a matter of reciprocal human relationships; the genuine relationship vanishes as soon as remuneration intervenes. The service of sacrifice cannot be paid, because paid love is no love; paid help no longer has anything to do with real help.

If we begin to understand the delicate relationship between 'service' and the social environment, new light is shed on a community with the task of educating and caring for the disabled. This work will only flourish if salaries are not involved. Payments should be made in another form. They can be given as freely as the services which are rendered.

In the economic sphere true brotherhood must reign – a brotherhood of inequality and individual standards. Not everyone can live under the same conditions as his brother and sister.

People's earthly needs are different, but people should learn to live together in fraternity despite their different financial needs.

There is, however, another social sphere where equality is necessary. This is the realm of people's individual rights. The right to speak, to know, and to do. A human community can only function if these rights are properly observed. Every area of work and life – be it a school, a business, a factory or a hospital – can only be permeated by the good will of everyone involved if every participant and contributor knows the work of the others, or is able to inform himself about it. Everyone must also have the right to give his opinion about how the work should be apportioned, organised and carried forward. Each voice must be heard. And, lastly, the opportunity must be given to each one to do the kind of work to which he feels called. But he cannot claim this right for himself without granting it to all the others.

In the realm of human collaboration and living together, it is the equality of rights – not brotherliness – that is necessary. The necessities of life are a matter of the individual, and depends on personal needs. and necessities. By contrast, the diversity of creative capacities, talents and work potential call for a sphere of common rights where equal justice is done to all.

A third realm remains in the social order; it is the sphere of independent cultural life. Neither equality nor brotherhood rules here. For this is the space in which the human being has to be antisocial and 'self-centred'. In our time, it is not possible to always behave socially. If we would do so, we would soon lose our identity and individual existence. Some sphere of privacy must be provided for each single person in a working community. Whether this is one's own bedroom or a family room for one's own family needs to be decided individually. One person will want to have his own workbench, another will want his own library, and another will want time for his own studies. Freedom should reign in this social realm – but not liberty alone. The individual must also allow his conscience to speak, so that his requirements remain in harmony with the needs of the community.

If, step by step, these spheres of social order are achieved and adapted to the living situation, order and harmony will prevail in the community.

Fraternity lives in the economic sphere.

Equality is needed in the realm of co-operation and work.

Liberty, accompanied by the voice of conscience, rules the cultural life.

In a community of this kind, the child with special needs will feel received and secure. The delayed and physically disabled young person will feel confirmed in his humanness, and every coworker can find a place where he can live and is able to work creatively. This kind of social order is the third essential of Camphill.

The interrelationship of the three essentials

These are the three essentials which give the basis to our life and form the background to our work. They indicate the difference between Camphill and similar schools and homes for children with handicaps.

These essentials are threefold in structure and it would be difficult to establish one or even two without attempting all three together. The three essentials are interwoven with one another. Regard for the spiritual nature of one's fellow man, the endeavour of one's inner development and the establishment of a true community are a trinity; they are a threefold unity.

This threefold ideal will hardly ever find fulfilment here on earth. It should be an aim we try to achieve and a goal for which we strive; but it lies in the nature of every ideal that it can never be fully attained. This is human destiny. Nevertheless, to attempt to find the way and to walk towards an ideal are necessary.

When this is done the right atmosphere is created, which is

a fundamental need for every person with handicaps, child or adult. It is an atmosphere of human striving and endeavour for spiritual ideals. These personalities need an environment which is permeated by higher values, spiritual and religious.

The child in need of special care asks for the renewal of his soul. But regeneration can only occur if the child's surrounding is filled with higher values like the three essentials of Camphill. A community longing for communion with the spirit provides the true living breath for disabled, ill and handicapped people.

The renewal of the soul by the living breath of the spirit is the ultimate aim of remedial education. It strives for the repeated presence of the Comforter, the Holy Spirit, who is the Healing Spirit. The three essentials are one of the means to create a social condition for the Healing Spirit to work. He has the power to make every child and every man 'whole' again. But 'whole' is not 'healthy'. The Holy Spirit restores the strength to take up one's cross and to walk along the path of individual destiny.

In a community striving for the three essentials, the words of John the Baptist can be heard: 'The crooked shall be made straight, and the rough ways shall be made smooth; and all flesh shall see the salvation of God' (Luke 3:5f).

The Birth of a Movement

From Vienna via Switzerland 1938

Austria fell on March 11, 1938 under the pressure of propaganda attacks from outside and betrayal from within by our so-called 'fellow countrymen.' The German troops crossed the borders and the government was forced to relinquish power. It was a pitiful and disreputable end. Thoroughly corrupt through slander and lies, Austria could offer no resistance and was defeated. On the evening of that very day, our youth group came together. We read the last lecture of the Pedagogical Youth Course where Rudolf Steiner speaks about the working of the Archangel Michael in the twentieth century, calling on young people to make it possible for Michael to penetrate through the death and decay of contemporary civilisation.

> The age of Michael who conquers the dragon must now begin, for the power of the dragon has become great!
> It is this, above all, that we must accomplish, if we want to become true leaders of the young. For Michael needs, as it were, a chariot by means of which to enter our civilisation. And this chariot reveals itself to the true educator as coming forth from the young, growing human being, yes, even from the child. Here the power of the pre-earthly life is still working. Here we find, if we nurture it, what becomes the chariot by means of which Michael will enter our civilisation. By educating in

the right way we are preparing Michael's chariot for his entrance into our civilisation.

Yes, what was expressed here lived in our hearts as a longing. This was what really mattered to us and what we were striving to achieve. We were surrounded by chaos, madness and destruction and yet a light that we could follow with courage and good conscience had begun to shine in us. The closing words of these lectures gave us strength and guidance, for:

> Their aim was that you should not merely carry away in your heads what I have said here, and ponder it. What I would prefer is for you to have something in your hearts and then to transform what you carry in your hearts into activity. What human beings carry in their heads will be lost along the way. But what they receive into their hearts, their hearts will preserve and carry into all spheres of activity in which they are involved.[1]

Those were the very words we needed that night. They gave us purpose, strength and direction for what our future should become. We – those present – promised ourselves that we would faithfully carry our resolution to build a vehicle for Michael – wherever that may be – which he could use to enter our civilisation. With this promise we took our leave of one another. We did not know if we would remain free from harm or when we could meet again.

Outside the city was raging; Hitler youth in their white stockings, men in brown uniforms, and screeching women all danced around the dragon. Yet in the midst of this insane commotion a flame had been kindled; a flame that was to forge a sword of peace that could, perhaps, also shine as a small light for future deeds. For behind the veil, hidden in the background of this event, was the blazing fire of the funeral pyre upon which Jakob von Molay was burned to death some

624 years earlier.* These flames and those of the other fires that consumed the bodies of the Templars emblazoned the night sky on January 25 – because this order had been in the service of Michael.

During the following days it seemed as if Vienna and her people were drunk. And just as it is with a state of intoxication, half the people laughed hysterically and the other half was overwhelmed with misery. There was something strange and cruel about having to continue to live daily life in such catastrophic conditions. I was often called out as a doctor during these days to attend to suicide cases amongst my patients. They opened gas taps, threw themselves onto the streets from the top floors of their houses, overdosed on morphine or even shot themselves and their families. One despairing act followed another, and the 'victors' did everything to intensify fear and confusion. They confiscated homes and publicly ridiculed and degraded people on the streets. The victims' fear was so great that they complied without a word. And it was through this utterly blatant display of brutality that another aspect of the Austrian nation started to become clearly visible. I too was seized by the epidemic of panic during these days. I saw how everything I had achieved – a growing seed – was collapsing into nothing around me. But my courageous and loyal wife stood by me and within a few hours I had surmounted this crisis.

My friends did not come to any harm and nor was their freedom compromised at any time. Moreover, my family and I were able to continue daily life without too much humiliation. The medical practice also remained unharmed. Nonetheless, each one of us knew that if we wanted to keep our promise we would have to emigrate as quickly as possible. But where were we to go? By that time German and Austrian refugees were no longer accepted by many European countries – they too were in imminent danger of becoming the raging dragon's next victims.

---

* Jakob von Molay, the last Grand Master of the Order of Templars, was burned in Paris in 1314.

As we did not want to be drawn into the approaching war, we searched for a place where, in spite of the pending catastrophe, we could begin to develop our work. At the same time we did not want to leave Europe because we were not yet prepared to flee. Consequently the Irish Republic was our first choice and we also considered Cyprus because refugees were still being received there. We believed that the governments concerned should be fully informed as to our intentions, and so, following many shared conversations and discussions with the friends of the youth group, I wrote 'a plan for the establishment of a curative education institute.'[2] This document contained the basic principles for such an institute, which, in part at least, we were able to realise later on. Our plan had been written with the contemporary situation in mind and formulated in such a way as to meet the conditions required by Ireland. Those who try to recall the situation in Europe in spring 1938 would have to consider our project as pure illusion. For at that time every European country blocked all possible paths to emigration. And now an entire group of people, most of them young and without a real profession or practical training wanted to start anew somewhere – albeit with a very unusual project. 'This cannot possibly be realised now,' was the daily assessment of the situation; 'it is an impossible undertaking!'

The Irish Government refused our application almost immediately; there was no reply from Cyprus. What was to be done now? Surprisingly, we never once became dejected. We had firm faith in our idea and most of us were absolutely determined to follow it through to its practical realisation somewhere in Europe. And so the group devised the following plan: Each one of us would make an independent attempt to escape entrapment in Austria; we would do everything to keep strong and true bonds to each other; and the first of us to discover a situation where we could potentially realise our plans would inform the others. This is how we ensured a common path of action. Perhaps the old strategic law of 'March alone; fight united' was behind our plan.

The friends' gradual exodus from Vienna began in early summer. One went to Paris; another to Prague; a small group was given permission to stay in Basle temporarily. The others fled to Milan, Zagreb, London and Zurich. It was comforting to know that nearly everyone had already left Vienna well before I could consider leaving the city. At that point my influential patients began to be helpful to me and by means of high level protection I acquired a visa for Switzerland. Initially my wife and our four small children were to move to Gnadenfrei (in Silesia) to stay with relatives until a new home could be found. We hoped that this would be possible within a few months: If there would be only one more opportunity to move freely again, our intentions could be realised. This is how vague and uncertain our plans were at that time! Everything was built on hope alone.

The torment and misery became noticeably worse in Vienna. The Party and the authorities soon began to pressurise me and I knew that I would have to act quickly if I was to escape the Gestapo's web, vanishing without a trace. An Italian patient who had become a family friend the previous year, travelled from Rome by car to help arrange my departure during those last weeks. Donna Lucia de Viti de Marco was still able to accomplish certain things that were now beyond my possibilities. Undaunted and filled with courage, she confronted the petty tyrants. We left Vienna together on Sunday, August 14. My wife and children stayed behind – being 'Aryan' they were still somewhat protected. Donna Lucia took me safely across the border. It was a miraculous crossing made possible with the help of a drunken SA trooper. I had made it to Italy, escaping the murderers' clutches. I spent a few days with Donna Lucia and her sister, Donna Etta in their country house in the Apennine Mountains. I was in a strange state of mind: tired, alone, without a tangible goal and therefore also without a sense of the way forward. Goethe once described this condition in *Wilhelm Meister's Apprenticeship*: 'The human being,' it reads, 'cannot be placed in a more dangerous position than the moment when – as a result of external difficulties – a great change takes place in his circumstances and he has not been able to prepare his feeling and thinking for this change. Then an epoch without epoch can arise, and the less that the person notices that he is not equipped for his new conditions, the greater the contradiction overshadowing his circumstances.' This 'epoch without epoch' had begun for me. As I had no means of supporting myself – at that time refugees were only allowed to take ten German marks away with them – all I could do was to watch as I was moved from place to place.

To begin with I lived for a time at Gwatt on Lake Thun where the Baroness B[3] took care of me – in her way, but generously. I met many interesting people, amongst others Carl Zuckmayer the dramatist, old Baron Andrian, in his youth friend of Hofmannsthal, and Hans Müller the writer. These people were also blind to what was happening in Central Europe. While National Socialism was certainly abhorred, at the same time they believed that the whole business would be over in a matter of months. This group was so naive that one of them – a Count M. – had begun to write a novel describing the love between a German farmer's son and a Czech working girl. He truly believed that his novel could prevent occupation of the Sudetenland countries! I mention this example in order to characterise how lost and confused the elite were at that time.

Not long thereafter I visited Arlesheim where I was received warmly by Dr Wegman but with the greatest reserve by the workers at the clinic and at the Sonnenhof. I realised that it would be impossible to stay there for any length of time. I negotiated with the director of the Swiss Epilepsy Association in order to secure a work position in their laboratory. As I had already been developing new ideas for the treatment of epilepsy for quite some time, and empirical proof and confirmation were still needed, I thought this would be a productive use of the time given to me. Soon after their initial agreement, however,

I was informed that there was no interest in my inadequately substantiated statements.

On September 20 I travelled to Paris to look for new possibilities. France appealed to me. I sensed that I would be able to work there and to bring our plans to fruition. There were not only cheaply available houses but also entire villages that had been left completely deserted. So I sent the first circular letter to the friends from Paris. While the letter offered only vague hopes, it was nevertheless positive about the possibilities for our work to develop in France. A little more than a week later the Munich 'betrayal' took place. The stance taken by both Chamberlain and particularly Daladier gave me much food for thought. Would France survive if it continued to ingratiate itself so intimately with the devil?

On my return to Switzerland I travelled to Vevey on Lake Geneva. One of my former patients from Vienna, a violinist, Bronislav Hubermann, had invited me to spend a few weeks at his home. I could find no peace there at all, however, and soon left again. It seemed to me as though a decision – a turning point – was imminent. Dr Wegman kindly arranged for me to give a lecture course within the framework of her nursing training and Dr Marti, my friend in Basle, organised a series of public lectures at the Bernoullianum. These gestures truly helped me to survive the 'epoch without epoch.' A larger number of patients came to see me and gradually I began to feel somewhat integrated with life once again. In mid-October a letter arrived from the British Consulate in Bern. I was one of fifty Austrian doctors who had been given the permission of His Majesty's Government to study medicine and work as a doctor in Britain. Was this the expected sign of destiny? I had personally never made an application to the British government. Who could be behind this?

I discussed everything with Dr Wegman and she was of the opinion that I should immediately respond to this helping hand stretched out towards me. Previously she had told me about friends living near to Aberdeen who were prepared to provide assistance to a group of refugees. She considered it vital that curative work should begin in Scotland, thereby fruitfully complementing the work that had already started in England. She also promised to give us as much help as possible. And so it came about that I travelled to Bern to collect my entry visa where I was given the assurance that all members of my family could apply for their visas at the Consulate in Breslau and would be able to join me in England at any time. The question as to who my benefactor was remained unanswered. Had the die been cast? This was on October 20, 1938, two months after we fled from Vienna.

From Switzerland to London

Courses and lectures in Arlesheim and Basle continued, and because of them and my increasing patient load, I became more mobile and was able to travel here and there without constantly having to pinch pennies. In Zurich and Basle I met some of my friends who had found their way to Switzerland. We were no longer alone; we now knew where we were all living and were able to discuss possibilities for our future.

The lecture engagements lasted till the middle of November. I still clearly remember the lunar eclipse on the evening of November 7. The pallid, brownish light of the luminary was eerie in the night sky: a threat of impending calamity. Many people had gathered in the garden of the Arlesheim Clinic in order to watch this spectacle. Two days later, a new storm of annihilation broke out in Germany: all remaining synagogues burned down.* Tens of thousands of Jews were arrested, tortured and beaten; hundreds were murdered. And still, no one really wanted to face what was happening. What could we even do? The west was still paralysed, and dismissed it.

* Kristallnacht of November 9/10, 1938 was a progrom against Jews throughout Nazi Germany.

Better news came from France, in regard to our plans. Maybe we should still try to do something there, despite the open door in England? I decided to travel to Paris again and, should that not work, continue travelling directly from there to England. In Paris, I once more encountered the world that was perishing. It rained patients, discussions and meetings. I remember one lunch, arranged by the Baroness B and attended by Alma Werfel-Mahler and the enchanting Countess Starhemberg. I met the editor-in-chief of *Le Matin,* Mr Sauerwein, who was an enthusiastic student of Rudolf Steiner, for long negotiations. I was the guest of several wealthy people, and the wide world was once more open to me.

But my predominant experience was the corruption of the French government departments and the police. An audience with the Foreign Secretary at the time, Georges Bonnet, to whom I presented our ideas, convinced me that we no longer had a place in this country. Across to England – that was the way forward! Destiny had spoken irrevocably and unequivocally.

The loyal Donna Lucia was in Paris with me, and helped me with all external arrangements. I had only a partial command of the French language, so she was constantly required to interpret. She was also willing to accompany me to London and to facilitate my first days settling in. On the morning of December 8 we drove to Calais, crossed to Dover, and passed the borders of the island nation unmolested and without great difficulty. In the evening, we arrived in London and I was received at Victoria Station by several friends who were already there.

A sense of safety and security came over me. The first, decisive step was taken. Perhaps the next would follow soon. I was expected here. I had permission to stay here. I had been called here. Instead of Ireland, it was now England, and was apparently meant to be Scotland. Many thoughts passed through my heart and soul. Why here, of all places? What does this land have to do with our destiny? These were the questions that were waiting to be answered. But we were now on solid ground. We had our feet on the ground again, and a new era could begin.

Kirkton House and the others who joined

Before the story of further events can be told, the group of friends travelling to Scotland must first be described, for now each one of us began to lay our personal destiny on the scale of our new work. Each individual connected with the common idea and imprinted it with their particular stamp. The progress in Vienna had required full commitment from each person. The group had become scattered all over Europe, individuals isolated and torn apart from each other, and would only come back together and re-form in Scotland. Some fell by the wayside on their journey, but others found their way to us.[4]

Peter Roth was already in London at that time. He had studied medicine in Vienna and had just been in the process of taking his final exams, but was unable to finish them. The new regime denied him access to the university. He was especially interested in psychiatric and psychological problems. He had availed himself of a comprehensive education. He was moved by strong enthusiasm for anthroposophic spiritual science, and he exuded a warm-hearted social strength.

He was married to young Ann Nederhoed. The two of them had recently met in Vienna. She was an individual who was to play an important role in establishing Camphill, despite the fact that she initially took part in our group work only sporadically. She brought with her an international past: her father was a Dutch merchant, her mother an English journalist. She was born in Australia, spent her first years in Japan, and later moved to North America, where she was raised in New York and Pennsylvania. She then came to Europe, lived in Budapest and Vienna, and was trained as a dancer by the famous Grete Wiesenthal. Peter Roth was working in London at the time as chauffeur for an old English pastor, earning his living in this way for himself and his young wife. On the side, both of them translated German medical books into English.

Thomas Johannes Weihs was Peter's inseparable friend.

He had also studied medicine in Vienna, and was primarily interested in neurology. As he was married to a young Swiss woman, he was allowed to finish his studies at the University of Basle. However, he was made to promise never to work as a physician in Switzerland.

Peter and Thomas were the Castor and Pollux of that group of young friends who had found their way to me in the fall of 1936. They were full of joy in their life and their youth. From the beginning, I felt a deep bond with the two of them, and this feeling of connection never disappeared. Together, they represented the element of constant loyalty for our mutual work. Thomas Weihs was still in Basle when we began in England, and remained there until just before the outbreak of the war. He arrived in Scotland with his wife on the evening that war was declared.

Carlo Pietzner also belonged to this group. He had studied at the Academy of Fine Arts in Vienna. He was already a talented graphic artist and painter, much prized by his teachers. He was an artist through and through, and has always remained so. He wrote poetry and novels, and learned astonishingly quickly to express himself artistically in English. He was a friend of Robert Musil in Vienna, and in Prague, where he fled in the summer of 1938, he had long conversations with Oskar Kokoschka. I mention this because a stream of modern art entered our circle with him. He waited in Zurich for permission to enter England.

Alix Roth, Peter's sister, was one of the youngest members of our youth circle. She was a trained photographer and had worked at a famous studio in Vienna, where she came in contact with the great and famous in film, theatre, politics and finance. This had taught her about human weaknesses, but she had remained quiet and lonely. Although she spoke little, a great deal of constancy and dedication streamed from her being, which lent our circle a strong cohesive force. She had gone to Zagreb, and had to wait till January of 1939 before she was able to fly to England. Her plane landed at Croydon during a heavy thunderstorm.

Sally Gerstler, called Barbara Lipsker since her marriage, was also in London. She came from an Eastern European Jewish family with many children that had immigrated to Vienna during the First World War. Her brother, a child with special needs, spent many years in Pilgramshain and later died of generalised tuberculosis. Barbara belonged to the 'old' youth group. Bit by bit, she grew to be a part of our community, and was often the bearer of the voice of conscience, which was decisive in helping us move forwards in times of adversity. At the time, she was engaged as a governess with a family in central England. It took some time before she found the opportunity to join us.

Alex Baum was another who belonged to the group of the 'old' youth: A kind person who had studied chemistry in Vienna but had not been able to finish his studies. He sat, or, rather, he lay in a Paris hospital to which a physician friend had admitted him, so that the immigration police couldn't deport him. His loyalty and steadfast dedication to our work was a great help. In later years, he was able to recast his extensive knowledge into wisdom.

At that time, Lisl Schwalb already lived in Scotland, at the house of a friend who had been recommended to me by Dr Wegman. She was a shy person, full of anxiety and reticence, who never completely succeeded in joining our cause.

Her friend and fiancé, Hans Schauder, was still in Basle, where he, like Thomas Weihs, was finishing his medical studies. In Vienna, he had been the focus of the old youth group. Ungainly in appearance, he had the gift of deep inwardness. He was strongly predisposed to retrospection, so he tended constantly to caution and forbearance. A contemplative melancholy, often paired with anxiety and resignation, made living with others difficult. He was one of the most talented of our youth circle, but had trouble proceeding from thinking to doing. After several years of honest effort to fit in, he and Lisl left Camphill.

Trude Blau was a curative educator working at the Sonnenhof in Arlesheim. She belonged to the first youth circle in Vienna, but went to Arlesheim at the end of 1936 and became a capable curative educator. Dr Wegman advised her to rejoin our group. She took on this task, and performed it with dedication.

In London I met Marie Blitz again, whose mother had been a patient of mine in Vienna. In a conversation that revealed to me the desolation of her existence at the time, I suggested to her that she join us. She agreed, and was for many years a very gifted, and often also willful coworker. We remained close friends with her.

I should also mention Willi Amann and Hugo Frischauer. The first was the son of an important father, and this destiny was a heavy burden for him. Only rarely was he able to meet the demands of life. As a loyal friend of Hans Schauder, he accompanied him as he began a new job in the region of Edinburgh. The second had suffered severely in a concentration camp. He had barely participated in our evening gatherings, and later, couldn't make up his mind to share our life.

The old nurse, [Sister Sabine] Pini, who had been a loyal friend and helper to my wife during our time in Vienna, remained behind in Germany. It was with great joy that we saw her again after the war. She had suffered greatly, but bore it all with dignity and strength. Rosa Brandstädter also elected to stay in Vienna. She was so deeply rooted in the Austrian folk soul that she was not able to leave her home, despite her close connection to our family and the youth group. Later, we often saw her again; for a long time, she was our guest in Camphill. A dark death called her from this life.

Still others should be mentioned who were involved in our preparatory beginnings in Vienna: The sisters Hanna and Hedda Förster; Eduard Weissberg, who now works in America; the engineer Hermann Meisel and his wife Friedel, and others.

Peter and Alix Roth's parents also directly helped establish us in Scotland, with great commitment. Emil Roth, their father, was a well-known civil engineer in Vienna, who had carried out large street and bridge-building projects. He was also a farmer, and enthusiastically farmed his large property, Schloss Kattau in

Lower Austria. He and his wife were now prepared to take part in our plans – more peripherally, but nevertheless actively.

This was by and large the situation I could expect for our coming work when I arrived in London. It was not as important that not all friends could participate directly. Their positive thoughts and feelings, their good wishes also helped to build the aura of the work to come.

A few days after my arrival in England, as soon as the necessary formalities had been taken care of and the first obstacles of strangeness had been overcome, I drove with Emil Roth, setting off from London to Aberdeen on the evening of December 13. We had been invited to stay for several days with friends of Dr Ita Wegman's, Mr and Mrs W.M. Houghton, for preparatory discussions regarding our future work together. They had a large estate north of Aberdeen, near the town of Insch, on the way to Huntly and Elgin.

When we arrived in Williamston the following early afternoon, we came face to face with a strange, new world. This estate was inserted in lonely isolation into a peculiar, desolate landscape. The manor house was a beautiful and simply designed building. The great park with its walled garden was the pride of its childless owners. Mr and Mrs Houghton belonged to the gentry of the area. Their farms were occupied by tenants, and there was a natural hierarchical relationship between the masters and the farmers and staff.

A tour the following morning revealed to me all that was there in its sleeping stillness and beauty. It was winter; all was bare and as if frozen. And yet I could sense the hidden magic of this nature. On the edge of the well in the dreaming garden sat an old wild duck that for years had made that place its home. I was suddenly moved to speak the strange verse from Hofmannsthal's *Lebenslied:*

> On peacock, lamb and eagle
> His youthful lordship brave

May waste the ointment regal
An old, dead woman gave.[5]

What did this all mean?

In the morning, as the master and mistress sat at breakfast, the old gardener, Mr Mackintosh, came in. He was given a cup of coffee, sat down on the corner bench at a befitting distance, and reported what he had done yesterday and what he planned to do today. Each day, he was told how many heads of cabbage, carrots, and Savoy cabbages he was to deliver to the kitchens. It had been the same number every day for years. But before breakfast, the house staff gathered in the same room. Mr Houghton read a short selection from the Bible, and then everyone knelt for a silent morning prayer. This was the world we encountered here.

Only on the second day were we led to the house that Mr Houghton was prepared to buy for us and make available for our work. It stood on a hill, at some distance from the manor – an old parsonage, unused for years. It was framed by a completely overgrown garden. Next to it stood a small chapel with a tiny graveyard. The parish had been dissolved, as the former community had been combined with another church.

Kirkton House

The house itself, however, was quite spacious. It had two large rooms on the ground floor, and several rooms on both the first and second floors. Although there was neither electric light nor central heating, and there was only a single, ancient bathroom, it seemed to me a quite suitable, even ideal, house for our beginnings. Finally, another roof! And a garden! Mr Houghton also promised us milk and potatoes as initial assistance. We had here the possibility not only of living together, but also of taking in about ten children. What more could we wish for?

Much sooner than I had allowed myself to dream, a house had been found that would serve as our first settlement: Kirkton House. I hardly noticed, at first, that the wind blew through the badly framed windows, that the doors no longer closed properly, the kitchen stove smoked as soon as it was lit, and most of the fireplaces didn't work. And I could hardly look this gift horse in the mouth. I was glad it had been promised to us, even if it looked suspiciously like Don Quixote's Rocinante. To me, this horse was a worthy and noble steed.

Mr Houghton promised to have the worst damage repaired as soon as possible, to build a new bathroom in the first story, and to install the beginnings of a central heating system. In addition, Mrs Houghton invited my wife and children to stay with her at Williamston until Kirkton House was livable. More than I had hoped seemed suddenly to have been achieved. Four months after our flight from Vienna, we had found safe harbour for our future work.

Preparations

Back in London, I wrote a Christmas newsletter to our friends and invited them to prepare for their entry into England. I bade my wife arrange for a visa in Breslau and organise her journey with the children as soon as possible. Although her parents advised her against emigrating to a foreign country in the winter, we wanted to be together again as a family.

On the evening of December 30 and the last day of 1938, I drove from London to Harwich. There I awaited the arrival of my wife and children. Dear Donna Lucia had met them in Flushing and now brought them safely to me. As the ship approached, Tilla stood on the deck with little Veronika in her arms. Donna Lucia carried Andreas, and Renate and Christoph watched all of the newness coming toward them with wide eyes. Late that night we arrived in London, tired but happy. On January 2, I accompanied Tilla and the children to Williamston, where they were received by our hosts. After only a few days, I drove back to London. Now, finally, I could put all my energy into carrying out the necessary groundwork.

Now began the many visits with pleas for aid to the various refugee organisations and to the British Home Office. A long list of information regarding our plans had to be submitted. The Quakers, the Anthroposophical Society in Great Britain, the Church of Scotland's Christian Council for Refugees, and several individuals helped us and supported our endeavour. There were many interviews and discussions that lasted until the middle of March, 1939. But then the Home Office gave us a general permit for our whole group of friends, making possible entry, stay and work for everyone within the framework of our endeavour.

As for myself, I was admitted as a student to the University of St Andrew in Dundee, so I would be able to regularly travel back and forth between Kirkton House and Dundee. The Church of Scotland took care of the finances related to my studies. Active support came toward us from many sides.

Dr Eugen Kolisko, who also lived in London and was working on establishing a School for Spiritual Science, also invited me to lectures. However, my knowledge of the English language was so meagre that I was not able to accept his offer. Instead, I began to write several articles for his newspaper, *Modern Mystic*.

He supported my plans in every way, although he had hoped to gain me as a coworker for his plans in London. I believe that it was also he who saw to it that I was one of the fifty physicians from Austria who received an immigration and residence permit.[6]

In addition to the many discussions and requests for help, a new circle of people also began to gather around me. Patients I had treated in Vienna and who were now, like me, refugees, continued to ask for my advice. But British people also came, and some days were quite full of consultations. I lived in a small room in London in a house that had been set up for friends through the initiative of Dr Kolisko. The Roth parents and other acquaintances were also living there.

I visited many physicians, to let them know of our plans. From most of them I received some interest and the vague promise to refer children to us in the future. At the time, curative education was not yet well known, and child psychiatry only a hope for the future.

In January, Alix Roth arrived in London, glad to have escaped her exile in Zagreb. Carlo Pietzner came to England several weeks later, and the first nucleus of a group began to gather. Preparations in Kirkton House were well underway; I travelled up in February to see how far things had come. Our furniture was on the way from Zurich to Aberdeen. My wife went up to Kirkton House every day, and began to plan the furnishings for each room.

In mid-March, Alix and Ann Roth drove to Insch to help with the relocation to the new house. And on March 30, 1939, on the fourteenth anniversary of Rudolf Steiner's death, the three women, with our four children, completed the move into Kirkton house.

On the same day, I left London with Peter Roth. We stopped first in Edinburgh, in order to negotiate our endeavour and its financial support with Church of Scotland representatives of the Council for Refugees. They knew of our plans, and promised generous support. We resumed our journey on April 1, and arrived at Kirkton House in the evening. After months of waiting, we were finally *home* again. We could hardly comprehend that the seed of something new was now a reality.

View from Kirkton House to Bennachie

The south-facing windows looked out onto the Scottish lowlands. From this plain rises the legendary mountain, Bennachie. It has a two-peaked summit with a strange contour. The first night in Kirkton House, I had a striking dream: I saw a great ship, which I immediately knew to be Noah's Ark, landing on the summit of Bennachie. It anchored between the two peaks. Then the doors in the powerful ship's body sprang open, and a great crowd of people – men, women, children, large and small, old and young – streamed from the belly of the ark. They moved downwards from the summit and began to populate the land. I awoke bemused and astonished: Was this a sign for our coming work?

Now the real preparations began. Early every Monday morning I drove through Aberdeen to Dundee. I remained there till midday on Friday, attended lectures in the mornings and afternoons, and strove to learn the English language. The students met me with reserved friendliness. They didn't quite know what to do with me, and for my part, I had little desire to develop closer contact with them. But some professors confronted me with badly concealed enmity. They saw, in me, the German adversary. However, others were friendly and accommodating. One close relationship developed with the Dean of Medicine, Professor Cappel. He taught pathology and pathological anatomy, and we had many lovely conversations. He showed personal empathy for my destiny.

This period of studying was a great blessing for me. I was finally able to read up on the medical literature of recent years at the university library. I heard of many new observations in the lectures, and was able to significantly expand my knowledge as a physician. I also had time to pursue my own thoughts again and to work through new ideas. I studied many lectures by Rudolf Steiner, and gained important insights from them.

I passed the weekends in Aberdeen and Kirkton House. There, my wife was the calming centre. She kept the house, continued to improve upon its livability with our three friends, and slowly managed to build the first nucleus of the community. However, a certain tension developed between us and Mr and Mrs Houghton, due to national and cultural differences. The two Scots felt obliged to oversee our work and life, as they had active feelings of superiority toward all foreigners. They often treated us as the English were wont to treat natives in the colonies. Grave misunderstandings resulted from this behaviour, and some difficulties arose.

However, we began to develop the consciousness within our group that we were a *community*. We shared all of our possessions with each other. We lived and worked together, and although it was not always easy to remain cheerful and relaxed, the feeling of brotherhood continued to grow within us. Only Lisl Schwalb, who still lived in Williamston, did not take part in this.

Pictures from König's photo album, captioned: 'Rudi Samoje and Peter Bergel came, livening up things.'

Beginnings of curative work

At the beginning of May, the first two children moved in: Peter B[ergel], a restless boy of eight, who suffered from the results of a brain infection, and the seventeen-year-old Rudi S[amoje],[7] who had epilepsy, but was a friendly and quite intelligent person. He loved his concertina, and played it often. We absorbed them both completely into our life-sharing community. They worked with us in the house and garden, helped in the kitchen, and were members of our growing family.

Rudi Samoje and Christoph König

In June, two more charges joined us: an English child with severe retardation, Robin L[eney], and a somewhat older Scottish boy, Sandy Th[ompson].[8] Robin was extraordinarily delicate and of fragile health – the last offspring of an old

English family. But Sandy was severely ill. He suffered from a progressive degeneration of the nervous system. Our curative education work began with these four children and youth. We started with exercises and an initial class. However, the social integration of these first four charges into our daily schedule and our whole life was even more important to us.

On Saturday and Sunday evenings, we coworkers studied the lectures from the Curative Education Course. We also read the *Chemical Wedding of Christian Rosenkreutz* together, and took up some of Rudolf Steiner's illustrations of specific questions in Christianity in connection with it.

In the meantime, the Roth parents had leased a beautiful property near Aberdeen – Heathcot House – and furnished it as a guest house. Several people with chronic illnesses settled there, and asked for my assistance as a physician. In this way, the beginnings of a small sanatorium business were created. An initially still quite unprepossessing practice also began in Aberdeen. I began to have varied work. From Monday to Friday I was a student and learner in Dundee. From there I drove to Heathcot, saw my patients there and in Aberdeen, and then spent the weekend at Kirkton House. There, I helped to establish the curative education work and to support the first steps of community building. Amidst all this, I visited London, Birmingham, Manchester and Edinburgh for lectures and meetings. In this way, Britain gradually became familiar to me.

On Whitsun, May 28, 1939, we officially opened Kirkton House and our work there with a small celebration. I spoke first to the children, then greeted the guests and friends, thanked Mr and Mrs Houghton for all of their help, and spoke the words of the Foundation Stone meditation that Rudolf Steiner had given us at the founding of the General Anthroposophical Society at Christmas, 1923.[9]

The children of Kirkton House, 1939. Front row (left to right): Christoph, Andreas and Veronika König. Behind them: Jonty Somervell, Renate König, Peter Bergel, Robert Leney. Back: not definitely identified, one of them is probably Sandy Thompson.

A whole series of Scots now began to hear of our work. Clergymen, physicians and other interested parties came to us with questions. In connection with this, we began to recognise that Kirkton House was actually too far from Aberdeen to develop more extensive curative education work. The guardianship of Mr and Mrs Houghton was also becoming increasingly oppressive. We longed to move on, in order to be freer and more effective on a larger scale.

More and more requests to take in children began coming to us at this time, but our house had become much too small. Marie Blitz and Trude Blau had arrived in the interim, and we were expecting still more friends. Now, for the first time, Kirkton House began to show its real shortcomings. Petroleum lamps and open fireplaces were a constant danger to our charges.

Would we be able to receive official authorisation to run a curative education institute under such conditions? The laws regarding such things were already at that time quite strict.

At the same time, the shadows of the approaching war became ever more threatening. In mid-March, Hitler had occupied Czechoslovakia and declared it a *protectorate*. His next goal was to conquer Poland. But the English and French governments still believed they could remain at peace.

At the beginning of August, 1939, I visited the summer school which had been organised that year in Cambridge by the English Anthroposophical Society. I met several friends there from continental Europe; we knew that we wouldn't see each other again for years. And at the beginning of September the war began. The lights over Europe finally went out.

The day before, Thomas Weihs and his wife had arrived. Alex Baum and Carlo Pietzner had also come. The latter, however, was staying for now with friends in the Lake District. Only Hans Schauder had stayed in Basle. But all of the others who wanted to be a part of it were now in the country that would become our new home and place of work.

With the outbreak of war and the immediately mandated blackout, a curtain seemed to be drawn around the island nation. Now we were truly cut off from all of our past, and had only ourselves to fall back on. But as a group, we carried with us the spectrum of an Austrian past. If we looked back at the origins of all our ancestors, we were descendants of all of the regions and countries of the former monarchy. Bohemia and Moravia, Hungary and Croatia, Italy and Styria, Burgenland and Lower Austria, and also, through my wife, Silesia, which had been part of Austria before the Wars of Austrian Succession. I only realised this fact much later; at the time I was not aware of it. But the fact that we were Austrians lived in our hearts with strong conviction. Again and again, we returned to Raimund and Stifter, to Ferdinand von Saar and Schubert, to Waldmüller and Anastasius Grün, to Gustav Mahler, Bruckner and Beethoven. We felt it was especially significant that Rudolf Steiner also belonged to our country. We often spent time studying his childhood and youth, and his student years in Vienna. We were deeply gratified to be able to call ourselves Austrians.

For the moment, life and work continued as it had done. But on September 7, only a few days after the war broke out, we received a letter from Mr Houghton in which he made critical demands of us. He demanded that he take over the entire financial management of our growing organisation, that only he negotiate with the relevant government offices, and that his wife have overall control of our educational and curative educational measures. Should we not accept this, he would no longer be able to back us with the authorities. What could we do but accept this? But we also decided to leave Kirkton House as soon as possible and find another place for our work. The supremacy imposed on us bore the seed of rebellion within it.

Step by step, the work now began to take shape. We needed to transform ourselves from private citizens into curative educators, working according to a program. This was not easy, as most of us had been students up till this point, with only a superficially organised schedule. Hardly anyone knew how to sweep a floor, make a bed, clean a room or do laundry. Cooking also had to be learned, so it was a hard school of self-discipline that had to be undergone. Spade and shovel, hoe and rake were also almost unknown tools for most of us. In all of these areas, my wife was the teacher. And our charges developed by following the example of their teachers, as they learned.

In late fall, we suffered a heavy loss. Dr Eugen Kolisko died suddenly and unexpectedly on November 29, 1939. He was felled by a heart attack. I only heard of his passing several days later, but was in a strange state of consciousness during this time. It seemed to me that supersensible impressions were mixing with daily experiences, and it was not easy to determine, precisely, the boundary between this side and that side of the threshold. I mention this because since then, and for many years,

Eugen Kolisko has often been by my side. He has long been beside me as helper, admonisher and brother. I know that many of the events that followed his passing were only able to take place through his advice and his constant empathy.

In these first months of the war, we did not notice much change around us. We were no longer free to travel at will, to be sure, and required police permits for longer and shorter journeys. Because Austria had become part of Germany and was therefore now at war with Great Britain, we were officially regarded as enemy aliens. This was made clear to us over and over, though never in a hostile manner. But we were kept under surveillance and closely observed.

My studies in Dundee continued, and the curative education work in Kirkton House began to consolidate. I gave regular lectures at Heathcot House, and in Aberdeen and Perth. I spoke about anthroposophy in various groups and associations. It was a good exercise for learning the English language.

For Christmas, we again performed the Nativity and Shepherd's Play in Heathcot, Williamston and Kirkton House. Numerous people came to see it. During the Holy Nights we read, with great devotion, Rudolf Steiner's lectures on *The Fifth Gospel*. It was the beginning of January when we first heard of Camphill. It seemed to be the ideal location we had been searching for. But how could we acquire it? The price demanded for it was unaffordable for us. I tried unsuccessfully to find people who might be willing to purchase this beautiful estate for us. It was wartime, and everyone was holding on to his assets.

During this time, Hans Schauder also arrived from Basle in Williamston. Lisl Schwalb had managed – with the help of influential friends – to travel through France in order to pick up her friend and bring him to Scotland. They married quietly, and remained for the moment in Williamston. Their relationship to us in Kirkton House was uncommitted and hesitant.

I travelled to London at the end of January and saw a whole series of patients, as well as parents, who wanted to entrust their children to us. The past summer, I had met Mrs Peggy Macmillan. She was looking for a suitable place for her adult nephew, who had a developmental disability. Now his father also came to me, and I promised to take in his son. Mr Will Macmillan very much wanted to entrust us with his child. I told him of Camphill, and he immediately promised to help us.[10] He would buy Camphill himself and make it available to us. He instructed his attorney in Edinburgh to begin the purchase negotiations. This took place, and only a few weeks later, Camphill was leased to our work community. The contracts were signed in Edinburgh on March 27, 1940. A few days later, I communicated our decision to Mr Houghton. We planned to move to Camphill on May 30.

On the day the Camphill contracts were signed, I had a very significant encounter in Edinburgh. I spoke for the first time with the director of the recently formed Iona Community, Dr George MacLeod.[11] He was an impressive personality. Like his father, he was a minister of the Church of Scotland, a fiery spirit who wanted to reform the religious life of the Scottish church from the inside. He had an exuberant temperament, great social gifts, and was suffused with truly European learning. At the time, he was minister in one of the worst slums of Glasgow, and was completely dedicated to his work within his parish.

A year earlier, he had gathered around himself a group of young clergymen, theology students and workers. They spent several summer weeks together on the island of Iona and had begun to rebuild, with their own hands, the ruined church and the ruins of the monastery that had been built thirteen hundred years earlier by Saint Columba and his monks. A strong ancient Christian streak lived in this very modern human being. For example, he did not want only Sunday to be holy: the whole of life and all work must become a sacrament. So his and his friends' churches were open daily, and open prayer services were held there every midday and evening for all who wanted to attend. We felt immediately connected to each other, and spoke together for many hours. A deep connection ensued between our two attempts at community. I was deeply moved by this encounter, and he also found it very fateful for himself and his aims. A few weeks later, at the beginning of May, I visited him in Glasgow and gave a lecture to around fifty ministers on Rudolf Steiner's interpretation of the Gospels. George MacLeod thereupon began to study anthroposophy. I will speak later of his important further adventures. Many years of enduring friendship continued to bind us together.

During this period I also met Dr Robert Dods Brown, the Director of the Aberdeen Royal Mental Hospital connected with the university. He was a quiet person who smoothed our way in several instances. He had, at the time, already established a very modern mental institution, House of Daviot, near Inverurie, in which occupational therapy and artistic activities did much good for the patients.

Some other important individuals began to turn up in our sphere. Our Scottish destiny seemed to be broadening and deepening. I was convinced that this was connected with our decision to take the step to move from Kirkton House to Camphill, and that the directing hand of Eugen Kolisko was behind it all.

A sudden unexpected move

Up to this point, we felt little of the actual war. But at the beginning of April, suddenly and unexpectedly, came the invasion of Denmark and Norway. This tore all of England out if its dreamy state, and we began to bethink ourselves and to notice that the war had truly broken out. A deep shock passed through all of the people. In my journal entry from April 10 it says:

> Everything in me seems to be stunned, and my feelings and thoughts circle constantly around the great battle that

is taking place in Norway. Incessantly, I feel the dying, the sinking ships, the crashing planes, and the angels that are searching for their people in all of this distress.

This battle, poorly and insufficiently waged by England, was lost. The first heavy blow hit the island nation.

Shortly before this, I had been in London; I travelled from there to Oxford, to welcome my parents, who now lived in nearby Fairford. I was glad to see them again in good health. Friends had made it possible to bring them from Austria to England. From there I travelled to Minehead, where I held a series of lectures for the staff of the Waldorf School, which had been evacuated there. I travelled back to Kirkton House via Bristol, London and Edinburgh. There were conversations, lectures and meetings in each of these cities. In this way, the sphere of our work continued to grow.

On the Friday before Whitsun I had the decisive meeting with our Aberdeen friend and attorney, Mr Downie Campbell, about our move from Kirkton House to Camphill and the necessary funding for it. He agreed to help and support us. On that very day, the German invasion of Holland and Belgium and their campaign against France began. The hell of war had broken out. The fronts of the western powers quickly collapsed.

But in Kirkton House, everything remained peaceful. We quietly prepared for the Whitsun holiday and on Sunday I held the Children's Service, in radiant sunshine and with uplifted heart. The Whitsun message resounded from the altar and filled us with great joy. Then we took a Whitsun walk with the children and adults. When we returned, we were told that Frau Roth had called from Heathcot to say that her husband had just been collected by the police. All men with German and Austrian passports would be collected today and detained. We took in this news with astonishment and mild doubt, at first.

But as we sat at the festively decorated dinner table, the police came and ordered us men to dress and pack our suitcases in order to be ready for the transport in a half hour. Stunned silence fell on the coworkers and children. We ended our meal and readied ourselves to leave. What would happen now? The policemen assured us in a friendly manner that this was just a temporary measure – that there were many spies who must be caught. We would surely be home in a week.

But we were confused and uneasy at this sudden intrusion. What would happen to our wives? To our children? Would we be able to move to Camphill? Or was everything that had begun now at an end?

In this tangle of feelings, we took our leave. Peter, Thomas, Alex, Hugo and Willi were taken away with me. In the waiting van, we found Hans Schauder and several people we didn't know. And so we drove away. It was a radiant Whitsun day. The land was beautifully abloom. Peace lay over fields and gardens, and festively dressed people went freely on their way in the villages. We drove north, toward an unknown destination.

Modern Community Building

Social and Economic Foundations of the Camphill Movement

The Camphill movement is a community of purposeful activity which has given itself the task of creating a supportive way of life for physically and mentally disabled children, young people and adults, in order to serve individuals who have special needs. As long as they are children, they need to receive education as well as curative, therapeutic and medical support. The educational component is continued into the teenage years, but gradually leads into practical, vocational training. For adults, active work and a rhythmical way of life are made possible by means of workshops that produce meaningful articles, gardens, work on the land, etc.

The fundamental social law

From the beginning, of special concern to us was the forming of a social environment into which these children and adults can be integrated. For 25 years and through ongoing change, we have tried to develop and improve these social and economic conditions. For a residential school for children requires other social conditions than does an apprenticeship training or a village community of productively working adults.

Moreover, the children, young people and adults under consideration here are disabled to the degree that they can neither attend a normal school nor a school for children with learning difficulties, nor can they later – with few exceptions – be integrated into the conventional work force. All of this requires conditions that call for particular provisions. Nevertheless, the universal laws regulating the co-existence of individuals must shine through.

When we began in 1940 in northern Scotland, we were so-called emigrants. For political and other reasons, we had to turn our backs on our Austrian homeland, and to bring to realisation somewhere in the world the spiritual ideals we had set for ourselves. We were twelve young people who had taken it upon themselves to not only study anthroposophy but bring it to realisation in a life of active work. The area of curative education seemed to us to be suitable for this also because some of us had experience with this, and the impulse to help and to heal was alive in all of us.

Right from the start, it became clear to us – as an isolated group in the context of an initially foreign country – that, as curative educators, we would have to find a way of life that would be appropriate for this. Since we were also totally without means, there came about, as though by itself, an initially quite primitive form of a community having joint belongings. The household goods that had been brought along, the books, and other possessions belonged to all of us together. It would have been intolerable and incomprehensible if one person were to have had a lot, and another little. And since we had no money, all of the work in the house, garden and fields was also seen as a shared task that had to be done.

When the first children arrived and we thereby had increasing income, it was again self-evident: no one drew a salary, but we instead lived together in a kind of simple family association. Not only possessions but also money remained shared by everyone, and was used in a way that corresponded to everyone's circumstances and needs.

At the same time, we noticed that it was suitable to the children who had been entrusted to us to be surrounded by a life of this kind. To the degree that their forces allowed, they helped out in the house and garden, acquired practical life experience that had hitherto remained inaccessible to them, and began in this way to encounter the realities of daily existence. Through those in our care, the blessing of regular activity was revealed to us. In those days we also understood what Pestalozzi tried to achieve in Stans, Switzerland: education by means of steady and necessary work.

In addition, it became clear that this kind of work done by teachers, educators and helpers can only be done in the right way when it is neither bound to set work hours nor compensated by a salary or wage. For activity of this kind cannot be remunerated. It receives its value solely of itself, and not from money received for it.

Implementing this way of living was easy to begin with. The coworkers were connected to one another in friendship, and because we were a closed community with little contact to the outside, we established a stable circle of people surrounding the children in our care. In this way we also had full trust in one another, which extended right into the financial conduct of the individual members of this circle.

Soon, however, the work expanded. Additional people, who were at first new to us, came to work with us and had to learn to embrace these social forms of living together and to fit into this. This was easier than we at first thought it would be. In this setting with children in need of special care, this seemed to be very feasible, as they motivated the reciprocal trust and good will of their caretakers.

Additional houses were soon added to the first one, and the larger the circle of coworkers became and the greater the number of children and youth grew to be, the more it was necessary for the work to become more specialised. Curative exercises, therapeutic eurythmy, school instruction, and artistic activities became configured areas. Workshops were created, as well as gardening operations, a farm, and much more. What had been something more general, in which everyone was willing to engage in all aspects of the work, now fanned out into separate areas. Most coworkers specialised, and only in times of particular need or transition was there a readiness to revert from the specialised to the more general mode.

How should the financial arrangements now be organised in order to take this development into account? From earlier experience, we knew that money had to be dealt with consciously, so that it retains its value and purchase power. Yet this is possible only when the overview of income and expenses is clear enough that this can be dealt with responsibly. Furthermore, we knew that money should not simply be thrown together. When that happens, then the necessary overview is lost. These were our leading thoughts; from here we moved to action.

Each house, whether large or small, became an economically independent entity. Income and expenses were not centralised. Instead, every workshop, every household, the school, the farm, and the gardens became self-sufficient operations. Those who worked with each of these entities were co-responsible for income and expenses. Only then did we begin to understand that by means of this arrangement, the usual situation of hardship and distress – which comes about through salaries and wages – is overcome. For in this way, workers and employees can become independent, economically self-governing individuals and groups of individuals. Anyone who wants to can become an entrepreneur and build a social community with his collaborators.

In this way the 'fundamental social law' can be implemented in an initial, if still imperfect, manner. This law was formulated by Rudolf Steiner already 60 years ago in 1906, and states:

> In a community of human beings working together, the
> well-being of the community will be the greater, the
> less the individual claims for himself the proceeds of
> the work he has himself done; that is, the more of these

proceeds he makes over to his fellow workers, and the more his own requirements are satisfied not out of his own work done, but out of work done by the others.[1]

This is a means of transcending the conventional wage system, for work is not 'rewarded' with money, which must necessarily lead to an unfree relation between employer and employee. As long as there were still servants and unfree individuals, work could be remunerated. Since the rise of the third class into the sphere of freedom, the working human being should no longer be paid. The free human being carries out his work not just to his own advantage but for the sake of what is achieved by his activity. The completed work is the true reward. A community of people who really want to be free can therefore carry out its work only by conducting itself in accordance with the fundamental social law. Then one's own work is for the benefit of the others, and their work makes possible one's own needs in life.

In our time, one must learn that this law provides the sole guideline in accordance with which small and large communities of people working together can be built. If this does not take place, consequences appear that are described by Rudolf Steiner. 'All arrangements within a collectivity of people which go against this law must in the long run bring about misery and hardship.'

And Rudolf Steiner very emphatically warns against taking this law 'as a generality of a moral nature,' and believing, 'that everyone works in service of his fellow human beings.' He formulates clearly and plainly that he categorically rejects this kind of watering down, and says:

> In reality, this law lives as it should live only when a community of people succeeds in organising things in such a way that no one can ever claim for oneself the fruits of his own work, but instead that these fruits

entirely benefit the whole ... What matters is that working for one's fellow human beings and achieving a certain income should be two entirely separate things.

Every physically and mentally disabled person can intuitively understand these requirements set by Rudolf Steiner. For the work that he does is a kind of blessing that frees him from the twilight of inactivity and from the neon lights of cursory activities and hobbies. For this reason, it was relatively easy, in the various centres of the Camphill movement, to bring to realisation one of the many possibilities that are in accordance with this fundamental law.

Our attempt is now to also introduce this in an effective way in our village communities, where there is productive work taking place in workshops, gardens and agricultural operations. And although we sell our products on the open market and thereby enter into competition with other productions, it is still possible to follow this law within the framework of our villages. All of the work that is done is not remunerated, and yet everyone has the livelihood that he requires, regardless of how much he produces. He works for the others, and the others for him. Reciprocal trust provides the basis for this significant social experiment.

It is clear to us that we stand at the beginning of this attempt. It demands that one not think up some rigid system that one then tries to justify. Each country, each social community, each type of work asks for living adaptation to the given circumstances and conditions. Yet the basic principle may not be overlooked: that work and compensation have nothing – nothing at all – to do with each other. Only when this separation is reached does one begin to fulfill the fundamental social law.

Once this separation is attained, one can introduce social threefolding step-by-step. Without these foundations, an endeavour of this kind would never succeed, because the coupling of work and compensation stands opposed to the configuration into the three spheres of social life – the free cultural life, the sphere of rights and the economic life.

We will now briefly describe how these three spheres are in the process of developing in the Camphill centres.

[The second part of this article (apart from the concluding lines below) consists of the section 'Establishing a community,' p. 134–38 of 'The Three Essential of Camphill.']

In Camphill communities, one tries to make this form of social life into a reality. It is still a beginning, yet is filled with hope and promise for the future. For what Rudolf Steiner once said to a group of young people in 1921 increasingly becomes the guiding star of our activity:

> In the future any task an individual undertakes will be a common task, and everyone will have to make common tasks their own. It will not work any other way. But we can accomplish this only through association, not through organisation.[2]

Address to the Tutzinger Stern

At the Presentation of the Gold Medal for Service to Humanity

Ladies and gentlemen,

Accepting this great distinction on behalf of my colleagues is a very special moment for me. It is an extraordinary honour that is being awarded to my work and to my coworkers. I had never thought to experience something like this. Now it is happening, and I accept it with great gratitude and great humility.

Ladies and gentlemen, I would like to say a few words about those whom you are truly honouring here. For you are honouring not only my work, you are honouring not only those who have carried out this work with me; most of all you are honouring those for whom we seek to carry out this work. These are the children, the young people and the adults that hardly anyone cares about. When we began this work – in Silesia, in Germany, at the end of the 1920s – very little was known about these young people. They were either hidden at home with their families or the government tried to help them. Special schools were established for those who were educable; but those with physical disabilities, who had handicaps, who suffered from severe brain disorders – of those it was simply believed: well, that's how they are, and there is nothing we can do for them.

Karl König receiving the gold medal of the Tutzinger Stern

A great man named Rudolf Steiner spoke at length about these people in 1924 and showed a small group of young curative educators and physicians the way to do much more for these people with developmental disabilities – with learning difficulties, and those with physical disabilities, for the blind and deaf – than anyone had previously thought possible. Enthused and inspired by these words of Rudolf Steiner's, this group of people began to concern themselves with those who had been cast aside – to educate them, to live with them, and to meet them as fellow human beings. To do what is written on the flag of your Tutzinger Star. That is all that these people who are mentally not completely healthy need: the warmth of human contact and the full commitment to help.

When a group of my young friends who were committed to

helping others were forced to emigrate from Vienna in 1938 due to the political circumstances, we promised each other that we would find a place where we could begin such work. Friends in Scotland provided us with a small house. There we began our activity. It grew markedly; more and more parents with their children as well as people seeking help with their illness came to us. It was exemplary – truly exemplary, the way the British government treated us, especially considering that we were, from their perspective, 'enemies' during the Second World War. They provided us with all of the necessities. With the help of friends, we were able to acquire houses for the work, and more and more children were brought to us. After the war, as the borders gradually opened again, young people came to us from all over the world wanting to be trained in curative education. Thus the Camphill movement began.

And now we can say that people with developmental disabilities who seek and require help are being educated, guided and cared for in South Africa, North America, Germany, Holland, Switzerland, England, Ireland and Scotland. We are able to guide about a third of these people back into so-called normal life. And for the others, we are trying to establish villages in which they can live as human beings, not as patients, but as citizens of the country in which they grew up and feel at home.

One thing above all has given us the strength to do this work, and I would like to try to describe it in a few words. It is true that humaneness and benevolence are wonderful ideals, but how is it possible to meet these ideals constantly and over and over again without losing one's strength to continue? There is only one way, and that is to develop trust in each other. That is one of the most important spiritual foundations of our work. We coworkers must trust each other. We must be open with each other. And we strive to be so open with each other that there is never the slightest wall between one and the other; when a wall does arrive, we try to break it down again.

But this trust also requires something in order to be renewed daily and hourly. And this trust can only be drawn from an attitude of conviction that there is only *One* who guides us, helps us, stands by us. This is what we commonly – and often so incomprehensibly – call 'God'. Faith in God, the conviction that we are nothing and the activity of the divine spirit is everything, and that we are able to serve it: This alone continuously renews our human trust.

And furthermore, that we know that One is with us, beside us, above us and for us daily and hourly: *Christ* our Lord. Once, when his disciples asked him why this person was blind (today, one could also say deaf, lame, developmentally disabled and intellectually challenged) and the disciples didn't know if this blind person or his parents were to blame for it, he said: 'It is not he who has sinned, nor his parents, but that the works of God should be revealed in him.'

And it is this that we experience daily and hourly with our children, with those seeking our help, with those who have been damaged: *that the activity of God is revealed in them and particularly in them and through them.*

That you have perceived this, that you have recognised it, that you were prepared to honour it, was a great deed of humanity for which I thank you from the bottom of my heart. I will communicate it to all of my children, all of my adults, all of my coworkers. Many heartfelt thanks.

Appendix

Fragments from the story of Camphill 1939–1940
Anke Weihs

It is March 1975. It is early spring in the North East of Scotland. Folds of grey cloud hang over the round-backed hills; the furrowed fields are invested with a peculiar porphyry light as though from within, the chill air is pierced by the sharp minor cry of oystercatchers as they veer down in their steep flight over the bare earth.

This year's March contained the Easter week and within the Easter week this year fell the ninth anniversary of Karl König's death – and the fiftieth anniversary of Rudolf Steiner's death. March has significance in the story of Camphill.

The annexation of Austria by the Nazis in March, 1938 turned thousands of people into refugees, among them Dr König, his family and some young people who had pledged themselves to go with him to whatever country would give to the little group the possibility of starting a new community – a community with handicapped children, the central nerve of which was to be the inner way of anthroposophy.

Refugees of 1938 had little choice as to where to go. Some countries turned them back over the German border; other countries made conditions of entry very stringent. Applying for permits was laborious and fraught with disappointments, and

APPENDIX: FRAGMENTS FROM THE STORY OF CAMPHILL 1939–1940

waiting often precarious, It was not easy to enter any country as an individual, let alone as a group. Some of the original Viennese youth group that had formed around Dr König went their own ways and never reached Camphill,

Britain at that time was the humane one of the European countries. British Quaker and other organisations saved hundreds of refugees from the fate of being returned to Germany, and individual British citizens extended invitations to and stood as guarantors for hundreds of Austrians and Germans whom they had never met to ensure their safe progress to Britain.

Mr and Mrs Houghton, the owners of Williamston Estate north of Aberdeen, were among those who extended such invitations and threads were spun which ultimately brought it about that the diverging ways of Dr König and some of his young friends from Vienna began to converge upon a bleak little manse on the Williamston Estate in March, just a year later. Dr König himself was one of the prominent Austrian doctors granted a home in Britain, but before his family and friends were able to enter Britain, months of effort, patience and anxiety had to be experienced.

On March 30, 1939 – the fourteenth anniversary of Rudolf Steiner's death – Mrs König, Alix Roth and I moved in to Kirkton House. When, almost strangers to one another, we stood in the chilly little candle-lit entrance hall that evening to speak a prayer together, past and future seemed poised on a knife's edge: our single lives, embedded as they had been in a seemingly secure European context, had come to an end. Our lives as participants in an as yet unborn spiritual adventure had taken their first infinitesimal but irrevocable steps into a more than uncertain future,

For in this very same March 1939, the Nazis had invaded Czechoslovakia, the event that signified a massive stride towards the Second World War.

Dr König and Peter Roth joined us a day or two later and we were now five. At the end of our first week at Kirkton House there was an eclipse of the sun. The silent, untimely twilight that spread over the land struck an ominous keynote that year. One's own little degree of awareness seemed to flicker like the flame of a candle in a blast. Out of what resources could one draw to be strong enough, indeed willing enough, to undertake something together which had no name, no contours, but which was going to claim one's total existence whether oho wanted it to or not? For no one should think that we were a closely-knit, rational group of people choosing the way we wanted to go. Rather some kind of spiritual suction drew us up and buffeted us about, shredding our little bits of accustomed ways of life, leading us time and again into our own darkness within the gathering darkness in the world outside.

But then the four König children came up from Williamston where they had been staying and a few weeks later, Marie Blitz joined us. The house was full of life and our daily existence together began.

Life in Kirkton House was rudimentary and hard. Fires had to be lit every morning, for there was no heating. Lamps had to be trimmed and cleaned, for there was no electric light. Laundry was washed by hand in an old copper outside in a shed behind the house. Cooking was done on a rickety paraffin stove, which maliciously poured out clouds of black smoke every morning.

For the most part we had come out of comfortable Viennese homes and the load of hard practical work was a new experience. We had to learn that every task had its own importance and that when it was half-heartedly or incompletely carried out, it came back on us like a boomerang. At times, it was as though the accumulation of forgotten or neglected tasks would threaten our very existence; one's own untidiness and indolence are impositions on communal life. Dr and Mrs König with their intense sense of order, cleanliness and beauty set us a high standard. We had an experience of disaster when we fell short of that standard.

For Dr König there was no fumbling or skipping lightly towards an ideal way of life. Each step had to be responsibly and circumspectly taken, and although at times one might have felt that the emphasis on practical things was irksome and overdone, in retrospect one realises that the so-called 'devotion to the small thing' lays the foundation for therapeutic morality and responsibility and that, moreover, the ideal is always inherent in each step taken towards it.

There was another area of labour entirely new to us: the labour of learning to live together, to meet anew every day, of learning to bear with and ultimately, to support one another. Very quickly we grew sensitive to the failures of the other, and highly sensitive to being observed in our own failures. Daily we perceived ourselves mirrored in the others and reacted in shame, resentment and opposition, but also with a first dim awareness of that element in essential human life which Rudolf Steiner calls the experience of the Lesser Guardian.

A man may learn to face his own Lesser Guardian in the privacy of his own person, but to live in community in any real sense means to submit to an experience of one's Lesser Guardian in the other, and to permit the other to experience his Lesser Guardian in oneself. Neither is easy. There is a long way to go before learning to love the other who shows one a truth about oneself and before gaining sufficient respect and tact to show the other a truth about himself; but these things were basic for what was to come.

A further area of labour had to be encountered: the labour of getting to know anthroposophy. Regardless of the long hard days of physical work, we gathered every evening to read and to study. At times, we were well nigh unconscious for sheer exhaustion and it was sometimes intensely cold. For often, the wind whistled up through the floorboards in the library, causing the carpets to heave great sighs at our feet, and the heavy quilted curtains at the windows billowed in the draught as we became stiff with cold. Nonetheless, we had our first common and formative experiences in the sphere of anthroposophy.

First children arrive at Kirkton House

At that time, Dr König was determined on taking a British medical degree, but that necessitated his going back to university like any green young student. To this end he left Kirkton House every Monday to travel down to St Andrew's, to return to Kirkton House the following Friday evening. This imposed a tremendous strain on him, on Mrs König and on us all. His departures as well as his returns were not easy. We had an intense sense of loss and emptiness when he left on Mondays, but were apprehensive of his disappointments and disapproval – unequivocally expressed – when he returned. So each week had its dramatic beginning and end.

Later, the absurdity of Dr König's going back to medical school became all too apparent and he ceased his weekly trips to St Andrew's. On the tenth day of May, just about six weeks after we moved into Kirkton House, our first disabled child arrived and with him, our chosen vocation advanced to meet us. It was a dramatic encounter. Apart from Dr and Mrs König, none of us had had anything to do with children, let alone handicapped children.

Peter Bergel who is still a member of the Botton Village Community,[1] was ten years old when he came to Kirkton House, the son of a German Jewish couple who had found a new home in the United States but, owing to the American immigration laws, had had to leave Peter behind in Europe.

Peter – barely able to speak, incessantly restless, his mind bent obsessionally on looking for cigarette cartons – was a thoroughly disconcerting new element in our lives and collectively we faced the enigma of his existence with an overwhelming sense of impotence.

But Peter was soon followed by our next 'child' with

APPENDIX: FRAGMENTS FROM THE STORY OF CAMPHILL 1939–1940

handicaps, Rudi, a thirty-six-year old German epileptic,[2] whose convulsions were so violent and elemental that they could be heard from one end of the house to the other. And somewhat later, Robin, our first English child, came to live with us. In due course we had twelve children at Kirkton House, including the four König children.

From the outset Dr König took pains to impress upon us that we were not out to create an institutional existence for the children entrusted into our care, but, 'take these children into your lives – live with them as fellow human beings.'

Our first celebration was the Easter festival. The reading of the *Chymical Wedding of Christian Rosenkreutz* as well as much house-cleaning and polishing had preceded it.

The highlight of the festival was the egg-hunt for the children within our little walled garden on our hilltop.

One morning around that time, I was dusting Dr König's crystals and books in the library, when he rose from his desk and beckoned me to the window. For some reason I missed the fact that he was about to recount a dream he had had the night before and assumed that he was giving me some information he thought I ought to have. 'See,' he said, and pointed across the land to the peak of Bennachie, 'that is where Noah's Ark came down to rest, and now when the floods of terror and warfare are once again covering the face of the earth, we too must build an ark to help as many souls as we can.'[3]

I was deeply impressed by the second part of Dr König's statement, but equally puzzled by the first part referring to Bennachie as the mountain upon which Noah's Ark came to rest, for I knew it was commonly supposed that it came to rest on the slopes of Mount Ararat in Asia Minor. But Dr König, like his teacher Rudolf Steiner, so often made statements that utterly confounded one's conventional ideas that I was quite prepared to believe henceforth that the spiritual and world significance traditionally ascribed to Mount Ararat in reality belonged to Bennachie. And when, a few days later, a perfect double rainbow spanned the skies over the distant hills, the grim little manse of Kirkton became hallowed, a chosen place, and our humble lives at the foot of the holy mountain, a kind of sacrament.

May 28 was Whitsunday, 111 years and two days after Kasper Hauser's sudden appearance in the streets of Nürnberg. Six children and fifteen adults gathered in Kirkton House for its dedication to the task of curative education. Among the adults were Mr and Mrs Houghton, Mr and Mrs Roth, parents of Peter and Alix, their vivacious Hungarian grandmother, Mrs Blum, Kalmia Bittleston, three other friends and ourselves. The four König children, Peter Bergel and Rudi made up the small gathering. Dr König spoke of houses being like heads. People live and move in houses just as thoughts live and move in heads. When a person has lively and warm thoughts, a light radiates from his eyes, which imparts itself to others. Then people live and work in a house with a sense of purpose and in peace with one another, something radiates from that house and many will enter the door and seek shelter there.

He then spoke of the two streams of Christianity – the southern and the Celtic. He felt that the Celtic stream was waiting to be re-awakened in Scotland and hoped that we would not live in our new country as foreigners, but would learn to act for its good in the service of the needs of its disabled children, even if only in a preparatory way. (Dr König often emphasised that we were only the preparers of something, which would later on be carried by others.) He closed the dedication of Kirkton House with the Christmas Foundation Stone Meditation. Thus passed our first Whitsunday.

Life at Kirkton House

Gradually and carefully, Dr König introduced the Sunday Services into the life at Kirkton House, although they were not yet a regular occurrence. But he also instilled in us a feeling for social events, and birthdays, wedding anniversaries and the like, were occasions for mutual celebration and joy. At festive meals we paid tribute to the particular person in speeches, which invested him for that moment with his own potential and true royalty as a person. These were unforgettable occasions and profoundly formative.

Every evening after supper we all went outside to play games with the children. Peter [Roth] racing over the lawn with Renate König, then ten years old, had to be seen to be believed: it had the mythological quality of Atalanta's race. Peter was 'head teacher' at Kirkton House. Every morning, you could find him sprawling on the dining-room table on his tummy, drawing fascinating and Russian-looking pictures with Renate and the others in their wake, or could hear his booming voice giving whatever instructions constituted this extraordinary 'school'. In the evenings, the children were told the Iliad and Odyssey over shoe-cleaning on the kitchen staircase.

But then, there was our own 'education', Dr König made us learn and recite long poems (in German) with accompanying

The teacher Peter Roth with children at Kirkton House

gestures. In Schiller's 'Cranes', the wanderer suddenly comes upon the acropolis at Corinth and greets it with an exclamation of delight. How many times did poor Alix have to greet Corinth and register startled wonder as she did so! We had to learn songs too, morning songs, evening songs, folk songs, and to sing without reserve and inhibitions on all occasions.

Not long after we moved into Kirkton House, we experienced that we were not the only inhabitants of the manse. There were others – unseen, uncanny, but increasingly bolder in their efforts – perhaps to drive us out? Every evening when we had gathered in the library to study, these invisible inhabitants, who seemed to congregate in an empty room on the third floor, began to come down the staircase, first of all disturbing the children out of their sleep, keeping us awake as well with their pounding up and down and their unseen hostile presence. Going along the kitchen passage to one's room late at night, holding a candle in one's hand which flickered fitfully in the draught, one felt that hundreds of eyes were upon one. Had one had the courage to peer out of the window into the dark outside, one would not have been surprised to see myriads of ghostly cattle or sheep staring fixedly into the house as though it were theirs.

Whatever it was, the trouble slowly became traumatic for children and grown-ups alike, Dr König resolved to do something about it. One evening after our meeting in the library, we took candles and mounted the staircase to the third floor, trying not to let our hands and knees tremble too violently, and stood in a circle in the empty room. Dr König read those wonderful Rosicrucian verses by Rudolf Steiner which refer to the three kingdoms of nature and the three realms of the spirit in man, the goodness of which seemed to sooth the wild spirits which had plagued us. From that moment on the trouble ceased, and from then on we closed each evening with a verse.

All during this time, Dr König laboured unceasingly, often travelling to London, to procure entry to Britain for about

APPENDIX: FRAGMENTS FROM THE STORY OF CAMPHILL 1939–1940

twenty of his friends, young and old, who had wanted to help him in his new venture. Prominent on the list drawn up for the Home Office was the name of Dr Karl Schubert. Destiny decreed, however, that Karl Schubert was to come to Camphill much later, in August 1948, shortly before he died (in February 1949) Heroically, he carried on his special class, attached to the Waldorf School in Stuttgart, during the Nazi period in spite of being Jewish by blood. Many others on the list came to Camphill as visitors well after the war was over.

Events leading up to Germany's attack on Poland were gathering momentum. Alex Baum, Trude Blau and Thomas Weihs were among those who managed to catch the last boats across the Channel to England before it declared war on Germany on September 3, 1939. Their arrival at Insch Station was a truly sublime moment, for they were our longed-for brothers and only now were we truly 'we'.

Our journeys to Insch Station to fetch our beloved comrades to Kirkton House were undertaken in a vehicle that had been donated to us: an ancient ice-cream van on three wheels, which even when it was empty, wheezed asthmatically up the steep hill as though at its last gasp. When it was Alex' turn to be fetched from Insch, it did wheeze its last gasp! The increase in the little group at Kirkton House added further dimensions to our life. Thomas took to the land like a fish to water and was wonderfully practical. Trude with her gift for curative education and her training at the Sonnenhof in Arlesheim was an example of how to cope with the children, and Alex with his training and gifts of mind enriched our daily life.

The day the war broke out blackout was declared as a stringent measure throughout the country. Up in our remote little manse, we did not possess a wireless nor did we receive reliable daily news. So in the evening of that day, our little house on its hilltop was ablaze with light, while all the other houses in the valley were darkened. Although we were finally put right by the police the next day, the image of our little house shining out into the darkness, not only of the night but of a world moment, remained inscribed in our hearts.

Two things were making it difficult for us to honour our undertaking to integrate into and become helpful in our new country. With the outbreak of the war, we, who were predominantly Austrian and therefore technically citizens of a Nazi-dominated country, became enemy aliens. And then, very early on, the relationship between our hosts, Mr and Mrs Houghton, and ourselves became strained. In their experience, we were carrying out certain ideas given to them by Dr Ita Wegman when she visited Williamston a year or so before. In our experience, the Houghtons were providing a stepping-stone for the development of a future movement of community with the handicapped. Besides, they were so very British and we were so very Continental. Misunderstandings hardened into antagonism and these antagonisms were incompatible with our innermost aims, which were to serve the dignity and the goodness of man in all people. With increasing force it dawned on us that we would have to leave Kirkton House if our intentions were not to be entirely suffocated. But where would we go?

During one of his visits to London, Dr König had been approached by W.F. Macmillan, head of the publishing side of the Macmillan family, as to whether we could take his twenty-four-year-old son, Alistair. But as an example of the congestion that prevailed in Kirkton House, the fact was that we had had to saw a section out of the shelves in a tiny room which served as a telephone booth, office, linen cupboard and ironing-room, to make room for Alex's feet! In these circumstances we could not have taken one more person in, and so Dr König's response to Mr Macmillan was that were he to find a suitable place with sufficient scope and land and help us financially to acquire it, we would take his son.

Early in 1940, Camphill Estate in the Dee Valley came onto the market. It had formerly belonged to Lady Aberdeen, but was now owned by a Mr Gill, director of a well-known paint firm (which fact was to prove a remarkable advantage to ourselves, for the paintwork in the house was in perfect condition!) Talks began with influential people and with friends as to the wisdom of our undertaking a larger project such as Camphill would imply.

In two's we travelled over to the Dee Valley to see the new place. I myself saw it for the first time on March 26 in a snowstorm. In those days, the east drive was densely wooded with beeches, and an incredible giant silver cedar stood in front of the main house, towering above all the other trees in the estate. (This cedar fell in a gale during our first Carnival-Fasching at Camphill in 1941, and the majority of the beeches on the east drive fell in the freak storm of 1953.)

In those days, Culter and Milltimber were virtually separate villages outside the city of Aberdeen, and farms surrounded Camphill. Lying close to the river, secluded by its trees, fragrant from pines and well looked after, it seemed paradisal after the bleak, windswept, draughty manse at Kirkton, and our thoughts and love began to circulate around the new place like bees around honey, although our actual future as enemy aliens in a country valiantly and single-handedly at war remained obscure, to say the least.

Setback and step forward

On May 12, 1940, we celebrated our second Whitsunday at Kirkton House. By this time, the Sunday Services had been established as the core of our festivals. It was a warm and sunny day. We sat down to our Whitsunday dinner around the big table laid with festive care. Outside in the world, the drama of Dunkirk had just been enacted with all its implications for the future course of Britain and the war in Europe. But in the sun-filled dining room on our remote hillside in the north, we were striving to grasp the meaning of Whitsun as a singular human event and were united in a strong mood of peace and light.

During the meal, the telephone rang. Peter went out to answer it and on returning to the dining room, he whispered something in Dr König's ear, and the meal went on. Then we had finished, Dr König said that the police were on their way to intern all the men; they had already fetched Mr Roth, and the other men residing at Williamston, and as he spoke, we heard the police van coming up the hill. One or the other of us had witnessed people being fetched from their homes by Nazis. The kindly Scottish police were considerate and apologetic and gave us time to pack suitcases for the men. But all at once, they went away with the men to some unknown destination. That Whitsun evening in Kirkton House was very still and it would not be true to say that we were not profoundly stunned. But we tried to carry on the life with the children in as full and active a way as possible, so as not to burden them with the weight of an event we ourselves could hardly grasp.

The retreat of the British Sixth Army from Dunkirk opened up the extreme vulnerability of the British Isles to a possible German invasion. In the next few days after Whitsun, our first British child was withdrawn. Others were to follow.

The move to the new place in the Dee Valley had been planned for June 1, Camphill having meanwhile been bought by Mr Macmillan for our use (we subsequently bought it from Mr Macmillan). But now that Dr König and the other men had been interned, our children were being withdrawn, and the situation in the country worsening, Camphill receded behind the horizon like a bright dream before harsh realities. But what were the realities of our own existence? Six women – Mrs König, Alix, Marie, Trude, Lisl (who became the wife of Hans Schauder) and I sat upstairs in the music-room around a little table in the light of a candle and struggled to find these realities. Reason wrestled with idealism.

Kirkton House was small, we were known in the district, the Houghtons supplied us with oats, milk and potatoes free of charge. With the two or three children remaining with us, we

APPENDIX: FRAGMENTS FROM THE STORY OF CAMPHILL 1939–1940

could with great care just manage to see our way until we knew where the men were and when they would be likely to return. Moreover, how would we manage without Dr König who had conducted all our business himself and who was the one who attracted the children needing help? The voice of reason was powerful. The voice of idealism seemed inappropriate under the circumstances and – did it come from a sense of frustration at Kirkton House, from ambition, from a craving for more civilised conditions such as Camphill would offer? Or did it come as a summons from out of the future?

In those evening hours upstairs, an archetypal struggle took place in the six women: a struggle to discern what was self-will and anxiety, what was spirit-will and courage. Reason and idealism were two extremes. It was not a question of which would prevail over the other. It was a question of abandoning one's own opinion and one's own strong feeling to allow the presence of a third agent to enter and reveal its nature and unite the separate hearts and minds into one strength and one deed. And so we resolved not to remain in Kirkton House, but to make the move to Camphill, which was ready and waiting for us.

By this time, we had had the first news of the men and knew that they had been taken to Banff on the coast and that they were as comfortable as circumstances would permit. Dr König had written that we were under no conditions to move to the new place, but when he heard that we had resolved to do so, he was overjoyed.

There was now a lot to be done very quickly. For the last ten days at Kirkton House, Trude and Marie took the four König children and the two others to stay with Mrs Roth who had meantime rented Heathcot House on the South Deeside Road as a private guesthouse. Tilla König, Alix and I, once again alone in Kirkton House, began to dismantle curtains, pack books, pictures, linen, etc. and prepare for the move. These days were like being on the open sea with a strong wind in one's sails.

195

On May 31 our last day in Kirkton House dawned, that is, I suppose it dawned – for never had we seen such a deluge of rain. And here we were, dismantling our little ark!

At a timely hour in the morning, the removal vans we had ordered from a firm in Aberdeen rumbled up the steep hill and into our garden. An army of stalwart removal men leaped out and entered the house to begin their work. A few minutes later, more removal vans from another firm rumbled up the hill and into the garden and a fresh lot of stalwarts entered the house to begin their work. Both armies glowered at each other in the tiny entrance hall, having realised that they worked for firms that were each other's deadly enemies. Together they glowered at us. It was tense. It ensued that Mrs Roth, fearing that we were going to be unworldly, had ordered the one firm, and I, on behalf of Mrs König, had ordered the other. The only thing to do was to make tea. Then there were several placating phone calls to Aberdeen and we all became friends. Small wonder that the house was emptied in no time, and the two lots of removal vans rumbled down the hill again in the direction of Aberdeen, not, however, before Mrs König had carefully instructed the men to put all the furniture and packing cases in the front hall of Camphill House, because some friends of ours would be coming the next day to help us shift the furniture to the right places. She was referring to an offer of twelve young Iona Community ministers who had heard that we were without our menfolk and contemplating a big move. Dr König had met the Rev George MacLeod, who had just founded the Iona Community, and for a while it looked as though the two communities might forge a brotherly bond between them.

Mrs König, Alix and I stood in the forlorn little entrance hall of the once again empty Kirkton House, waiting for a taxi to take us to the station in Insch. Outside, the deluge continued unabated; water ran in rivulets everywhere. It was as though we were being washed away from that place.

APPENDIX: FRAGMENTS FROM THE STORY OF CAMPHILL 1939–1940

The move to Camphill

The next day – June 1, 1940 – really dawned. There was not a cloud in the sky. Tilla König, Alix and I went over to Camphill early in the morning. Our furniture, packing cases and other belongings were so tightly fitted into the entrance hall that we could hardly edge our way into it. But we made plans as to where the furniture should go and waited for the twelve ministers to arrive. We waited – and waited – and waited: the day passed without them. Nor did they come the next day or the next. They didn't come at all. We concluded that there had been a misunderstanding.

But the furniture stood in the entrance hall of Camphill House like an accumulation of druidical monoliths. So Alix and I, inspired by Tilla, began to shift it, not without long strategical arguments as to which end first. One evening at 11.30, we moved an enormous and solid cupboard down the long drive to the Lodge on a wheelbarrow. It was one of those long light Scottish summer nights. Imbued with some kind of superhuman strength that was not our own, we had shifted furniture all day. Finally, we reached the Lodge and unloaded the cupboard. Down the drive came Mrs König to inspect our labours, saying she was too tired to walk up the drive again. So we put her into the wheelbarrow and wheeled her home, stopping every few yards, bent double and helpless with laughter. In fact, at the sight of any enormous cupboard or other ponderous piece of furniture, we first dissolved in convulsions before we finally began to heave.

About ten days later, Trude, Marie and the children joined us, and a new era in our history began. Looking back, Dr König often remarked that Kirkton House was the embryonic period of what later became 'Camphill', and as menfolk are usually absent when a child is being born, so our men were absent when the move to Camphill took place, absent too, for the first few months of the newborn infant.

Camphill in those first few summer weeks was indeed like a bright and tender dream. It received us gently. We discovered its trees, the flowers, roses, an apple tree that actually bore big yellow apples, and each day brought us new delight. Every morning, we were greeted by a little robin which hopped in and out of the kitchen window, freely helping himself to our butter rations, and who turned up again in the garden, where we often worked until midnight. Yet there were sombre undertones. German bombing attacks against Britain began in the North-East. Notably in and around Aberdeen. A church in Garden Place was destroyed; a school received a direct hit with the loss of the lives of over a hundred children. German planes discharged their bombs in the fields around Cults on their way out to the sea, and air-raid warnings were a daily event. And – we were enemy aliens, and a regulation had been issued that no enemy aliens were to be allowed to remain within ten miles of the surrounding coastline [Camphill is 8 miles from the coast]. Whenever we answered the doorbell to an army or police officer, we expected to be told we would have to move. At the same time, the air force was requisitioning mansion houses to accommodate personnel, and air force officers frequently came to inspect Camphill House. We lived on trust that things would go the way they had to go.

Meanwhile, we had begun to receive regular letters from the men in camp and learned that after spending a fortnight in a castle in Banff, they had been moved to a transit camp in Liverpool, and from there, to the Isle of Man where they were accommodated in boarding-houses, for want of other camp accommodation. Peter and Thomas acted for a while as medical orderlies in the camp, but otherwise, the men's time was their own. Their letters were censored, but reassuring. They contained modest requests for sweets, clothing, books, drawing paper and coloured pencils. It was in camp that Dr König drew his illustrations to the fifty-two verses of the Calendar of the Soul, and Peter his striking illustrations to the Dream Song of Olaf Åsteson.[4]

Karl König's picture for the 23rd week (Sep 8–14) of the Soul Calendar. It is the only picture that seems to be 'autobiographical', showing him with his daughter Renate perhaps looking towards Bennachie.

It became apparent that our men were making the most of their enforced seclusion. Dr König, Dr Ernst Lehrs and Willi Sucher, an astronomer, conducted a kind of daily 'university' in anthroposophy and in esoteric life for their younger friends in camp. They worked through a study of the twelve senses and other basic fields of spiritual science, and many of the foundations of the spiritual and therapeutic life of Camphill were laid. We women in Camphill lived from letter to letter and from the calm and positivity that came from the men. I suppose they in turn lived from our reports as to how the work was being carried on in Camphill. For – in spite of Dr König's absence and the generally difficult times, some children had begun to come to us. Visitors came too, and the scope of our life increased.

St John's was fittingly our first festival in Camphill with its message: change yourselves. And soon afterwards there came a letter from Dr König saying that at Michaelmas there was to be a stellar constellation connected with John the Baptist and suggesting that Mark 6:14–44, should be read in preparation. And it was on August 29 of that year – on the day of the beheading of John the Baptist – that Dr König had his powerful dream-experience described in his *History of the Bible Evening*. Thus the peculiar quality of John the Baptist was woven into the texture of the very beginnings of Camphill.

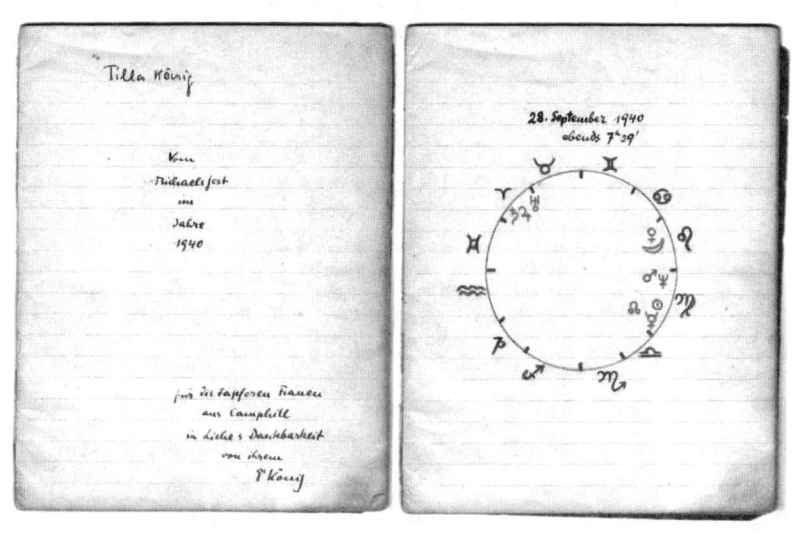

The cover of König's 'letter' (it was actually a little booklet) 'To the courageous women', and the horoscope drawing[5]

APPENDIX: FRAGMENTS FROM THE STORY OF CAMPHILL 1939-1940

For some time we had been negotiating with the Church of Scotland for a grant from a fund set up to aid refugees from Nazi oppression, the Scottish section of which was being administered by the Church. After providing statements and memoranda regarding our situation and intentions to work with disabled children, Dr König had received word that we were to be granted £1,000 from this fund, which was a sizeable sum of money in those days. Later it ensued that the £1,000 were to be shared with Mr and Mrs Roth and their guest-house. Still later, it turned out that the sum was not only to be divided between us, but that it was by no means a donation and would have to be repaid over a period of time. Meanwhile the Church of Scotland had appointed a local Aberdeen man to hold our share, £600, on our behalf. This man was J. Downie Campbell.

The arrangement the Church made with him was that we were required to list any needs we had and present the list to Mr Campbell. He would then procure what we required. Thus, if we needed pillow-slips, Mr Campbell bought pillow-slips and had them delivered to us. With growing numbers, we soon needed a considerable amount of crockery and we applied to Mr Campbell for leave to buy it ourselves. Instead, Mr Campbell went ahead and bought an enormous set of white china with gold rims – soup tureens, fish-plates, etc., all very fragile, virtually putting a china shop into the bull's pen. Our indignation was aroused by this slight to our freedom and dignity and the china was returned to Mr Campbell. The talks in his office that resulted from this incident laid the first foundations for the long relationship and friendship between Mr Downie Campbell and Camphill.

Meanwhile, all kinds of news was coming from the camp: the men were being sorted out, some were to be released, and unmarried men were being sent overseas to Canada and Australia. Alex just missed being included in a group of internees on their way to Canada in the *Arandora Star,* which was torpedoed in the Bristol Channel and went down with a tremendous loss of lives. We ourselves were busy writing petitions to the Home Office and other official bodies on behalf of Dr König and the other men. It appeared that those who had resided in England were being released at a quicker rate than those who had been interned in Scotland. Now that release was being spoken of, the pendulum between hope and despair swung more perceptibly towards hope.

The men return

Dr König got news of his impending release before Michaelmas and we counted on his being with us at Camphill for that festival. However, there were many formalities to be encountered before a person was actually cleared for release, and we ourselves had to attend a kind of tribunal at the City Police in Aberdeen on behalf of each of the men. Dr König was released on October 3, 1940, Thomas a little later, then Hans, and Peter only in February 1941. Carlo Pietzner, who had not yet been in Camphill but was in the country, was sent overseas. The other unmarried men, too, returned to freedom later by devious routes.

Dr König's arrival at Camphill was a wonderful and trying event at the same time. He was a man returning to freedom after some months in internment camp. He was a man returning to his wife and four children. He was returning to the main stream of his life and activity. But he was not returning to Camphill, for he had not yet been in Camphill. Although the women had taken over Camphill on his behalf, the move there had been theirs. In the few months we had lived together in Camphill we had begun to establish ways of living and coping with our daily situation. Whereas the men had been able to devote themselves in a unique way to spiritual life in the camp, the women had stoked boilers, washed laundry, tended children, and worked the garden. We had been living in two very different worlds. And so Dr König's coming constituted a stormy wedding feast between the male and female components of our community. But it was a valuable experience. Looking back, it would appear that basic to the well being of any community is the recognition of, and balance between the archetypal male and female elements.

Just about that time, the German attacks on Britain switched to England, and Coventry became the first serious target for bombing raids. Scotland from then on remained unscathed and with this, our own status as enemy aliens living in a coastal area became insignificant.

With the return of Thomas and Hans, we began the business of building up the community, for it was only then that we actually began to use the word community in reference to ourselves. One might say that the movement was born and christened with the move to Camphill, and that our inner striving likewise emerged and was christened when we began to say the Community.

As summer mellowed into late autumn, our life, which now included the men, began to mellow and assume deeper dimensions. We met every evening until very late to discuss matters ranging from the broom-and-dustpan, arrangements of rooms, to our spiritual life, and began to know and to recognise one another. In one of those early meetings, Dr König brought forward very tenderly his experience of August 29 and suggested that we try to institute a Bible Evening as a focal point in our life. Our reactions were partly dull, partly stunned and partly negative. None of us was really able to take the leap required to do what Dr König was proposing. The matter lay dormant for almost a year and then one of us suddenly asked, 'What was that you were talking about a year ago, Dr König?' And so we began our first tentative attempts to have a Bible Evening. But that was in 1941.

During the remainder of 1940, which for us had begun in Kirkton House, but which was to see us well into Camphill, amidst the increasing gravity of the European situation, our little group sat together night after night (in those days our meetings always began at 10 pm) kneading the dough of our existence.

Already then, the question of a threefold social order was raised, but Dr König refused to countenance any arbitrary application of Rudolf Steiner's social ideas to our hardly-budding community. We first had to find and experience a threefoldness in ourselves and in our children before we could speak of a social organism. Nonetheless, it was during this autumn that we discussed the question of the compatibility of taking salaries with our spiritual-social intentions and came to the conclusion that to work for salaries would obscure our perception of the image of the human being in each other.

Advent that year was dark inside and outside. Much of free Europe had been overrun by Germany. Inside, tiredness, frailty and some human difficulties had rendered us dull in consciousness and often it seemed we were trying to run a race with our feet glued to the ground. Dr König often withdrew from us in great gloom. But we performed the Nativity Play in front of ninety(!) people in Camphill House on December 22, on which evening Dr König spoke about the two Jesus children, which had a profound impact on those of us who heard these things for the first time. We had a beautiful Christmas Eve celebration and Midnight Service, and began the Holy Nights with a study of the lecture cycle on the folk souls, and our Advent gloom was dispelled in light and peace. Barbara arrived on December 30, and so one more of our number was with us to walk into the coming year.

W.F. Macmillan and the beginnings of Camphill

Our friend and benefactor, William F. Macmillan, died on May 11, 1954. A gentle spirit and a noble soul have left this earthly abode and a frail body after many years of physical and mental suffering.

His name will be united with the history of our schools as long as the work will be remembered. Even the date of his death is significant for his deep alliance with Camphill.

I remember very clearly May 11, 1940, fourteen years ago. It was a radiant day, the Saturday before Whit-Sunday. We were a small group of people and a very small number of children, preparing ourselves for the Whitsun Festival. The events of the war overshadowed life. The German army had just begun to invade Holland and Belgium, threatening France and Britain. More than a year previously, we had escaped the menacing power of nationalistic evil and found a home and work in Scotland. The manse of Kirkton near Insch in Aberdeenshire had been put at our disposal by friends. It was an old house with neither electric light nor heating, but for the beginning, it sheltered us and the few children we were able to take there.

Then at this Whitsun of 1940, we were looking forward to a great new step: to moving into a large and very suitably equipped house in the Dee valley a few miles from Aberdeen.

This new house was Camphill House. It had been bought by Mr Macmillan and, in a most generous way, handed over to us for a nominal rent.[6] Thus we, a small group of people who had decided to devote our lives to curative education, were given the possibility to go on with our work on a considerably greater scale. Mr Macmillan had faith in our aims and efforts. He did not ask for any security, he did not seek any benefit for himself.

He bought Camphill to serve a cause of which he knew little, but in which he had confidence.

I had met him in London a few months before; a frail figure with a finely-cut face. He was shy and reserved, and he had the great quality of being able to listen with care and interest to what another person had to say. He came to see me because he wanted my advice and help. He went away having offered to help us in the cause we were trying to serve. He proposed buying a house for us, should we find a suitable one. We found Camphill, and Mr Macmillan bought it.

On May 11, 1940, the scene was set for us to move to Camphill with our children. On the following day, our hopes were crushed – for on that day, all the men were interned for security reasons, being regarded as enemy aliens. At this stroke of destiny, the question of what would happen to Camphill was uppermost in our minds.

At the beginning of the internment there was little possibility of communication with the women we had left behind. We, the men, were filled with anxieties and fears as to whether they would be able to carry on the work. How would they be able to move into Camphill House without our help? Should they not move, or should they? Soon they too would be interned like us, and how then could the work proceed? The typical thoughts and emotions of those who are cut off from ordinary life overcame us. The clouds of the war had indeed descended.

Our women had more courage: they decided to move to Camphill as planned, and sought Mr Macmillan's consent to their bold intention. On the last day of May 1940, the women together with the children under their care, moved into Camphill House. They started to work in the garden, to look after the children, and to prepare for our return.

It was not until the autumn of that year, that some of the men were discharged from internment camp. Upon our return, we found Camphill waiting for us; the work could start afresh. Greater numbers of children began to arrive. This first winter was hard. The threat of invasion was present; the nights of bombing, though not directly experienced, cast their shadow over the land. But in the spring of 1941, the immediate danger seemed to be overcome and now a flow of children entered the gates of Camphill. The cottage was rebuilt for the purpose of housing children, and in that year, we had the first visit of Mr Macmillan.

He did not know Camphill, and saw it now for the first time. I showed him through the house, walked with him through the grounds, and he seemed to be satisfied with all he saw. He was far from acting as the owner. He was like a guest, gentle, reserved, yet open to the possibilities of the venture towards which he had so generously contributed.

He visited Camphill again in the course of the following years on two or three occasions. Later, travelling became too difficult for him, and the North-East of Scotland did not see him any more.

I was permitted to visit him three times during the later years. I found him struggling with the burden of his illness, yet his kindly spirit shone through the frailty of his body. He always asked about Camphill and its further development, and I was glad to be able to tell him of its growth.

When remembering Mr Macmillan, and trying to form an image of his personality, I see him as a gardener, quietly preparing the ground, digging, raking, weeding, watering, without pretension or pride, but with calm faith in the divine order of all life and existence.

In 1945 Mr Macmillan for a second time gave his help for the further growth of Camphill. A small estate with many buildings and a farm became available. It seemed to be an ideal place for the delinquent and maladjusted boys which came to us in ever increasing numbers. Mr Macmillan helped us acquire Newton Dee Estate. Thus he prepared another bed for a seed which has since grown and unfolded. Newton Dee is now a growing village with workshops of various kinds, and a well-stocked farm. There milk and bread are produced for all the houses of Camphill; the workshops turn out beds, tables, lockers and other furniture for the school; our shoes are repaired in Newton Dee, our cups and saucers, pots and plates are made in the pottery. But the most important thing in Newton Dee is the benefit our boys derive from the daily work on the farm and in the workshops.[7]

All this is due to W.F. Macmillan. His generous and helping hand was open to give; and fourteen years after the starting of Camphill, this hand was laid down to rest in peace.

His spirit accompanies our efforts from the farther side of existence. We shall continue to try and be worthy of his help and the trust he had in our work. We shall never let May 11 pass by without paying tribute to our great friend.

Karl König's star chart drawing
Alan Thewless

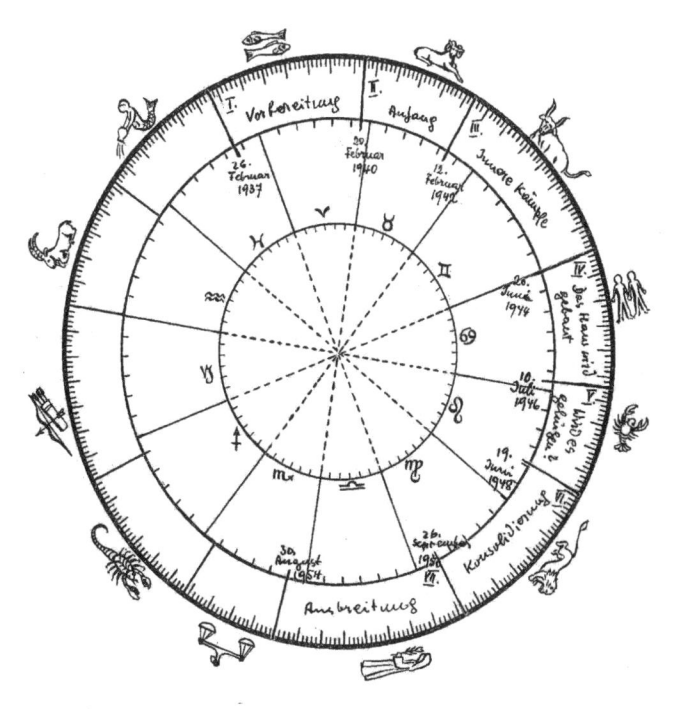

In this chart Karl Koenig is drawing attention to the movements of the planet Saturn through the constellations of the zodiac from February 26, 1937 to August 30, 1954. Saturn takes around 29.5 years to complete its round of the whole zodiac, so here we are looking at the planet's movements through seven constellations. On the inner circle the tropical 'signs' of the zodiac are marked whereas the pictures at the outer circle mark the constellations of stars. The dates indicated refer closely to points where Saturn made ingress into each constellation (not exact but close). These points indicate changes in emphasis and changes in opportunity, all closely linked to the unfolding of karma and spiritual pre-intentions, themes carried by the consciousness of Saturn. These subjects are clearly 'hovering' in Karl König's contemplations as he formulates the drawing.

Saturn is the planet of sublime historic conscience. Its passage through the constellations brings forth memories of all that has been inspired from these constellations and has been inscribed in them from world events since the beginning of time. Karl König is therefore looking at the birth and early development of the Camphill movement within this cosmic context of the Saturn script. He is seeing it in the context of the unfolding of world destiny (something traced by the movements of Saturn as mentioned above).

The sevenfold passage of the Sun from Pisces the Fishes to the Virgin marks the seasonal progression from spring to autumn (with an initial preparatory stage at the end of winter) and we can see that Saturn, in the drawing, is therefore tracing these same archetypes belonging roughly to new birth, through growth, maturity, blossoming, fruiting, regeneration – parallels will have been in Karl König's mind.

Contemplation becomes more specific, but still connected to the archetypes, with the designations:

1. Preparation
2. Begin
3. Inner battles
4. Building of the house
5. Will it succeed?
6. Consolidation
7. Spreading out

APPENDIX: KARL KÖNIG'S STAR CHART DRAWING

In the chart we have an opportunity of glimpsing an expansive contemplation pertaining to the beginnings of Camphill. The backdrop of time, especially in the earlier years, was one that also traced a period where the greatest destructive forces were unleashed against the human spirit. This must have been ever in Karl König's thoughts for this same period was one in which Saturn carried a mighty destiny motif belonging to the rebirth of etheric cognitive faculties and indeed perception of the etheric Christ. On several occasions Rudolf Steiner spoke about the significance of the 1930s and 1940s in this respect. How did this important theme and possibility weave into the unfolding of Camphill during this period? Was Karl König also tracing this in the chart? When it comes to Saturn we are obliged to look at the most serious considerations, something that Karl König was acutely aware of because of his intimate relationship with the planets and it seems specifically because of his awareness of the mysteries of Saturn.

Notes of a lecture in Sheffield

Lecture, <u>Sheffield</u>, May 10th, 1945

I.
1.) Not able to give a fair picture in a single lecture. Ideals & facts are mixed. I shall try to point out what differs at Camphill from other institutions of this type.

2.) "School for children in need of special care". It is a School & not a Home, this is because we are convinced that the greatest number of these children can be educated.

3.) "Special care": They are not backward or defective, but in need of special care, because they are different from the usual child.

II.
1.) The History of Camphill.
Austria – Europe – Scotland.

2.) The Place.
Camphill – Murtle – Heathcot

3.) The children
All types, ages, degrees of abnormality. Epileptics, spastics, feeble-minded, backward, moral insanity a.s.o.

III.
1.) The Staff. Community. No one is paid. No servants.
All work is done by the teachers & children together.

2.) The child lives with & in the Community. The life of the child is immersed in the life of the teacher & the Community of teachers.

3.) The child is filled with the conviction that he is a useful human being & that nothing is wrong with him.

IV.
1) The daily routine
   Its necessity.
2) The School.
   Periodical instructions.
   Artistic life.
   Work in House & out-doors.
3) The Story-lesson
   The religious life.

V.
1) The College-meeting.
   The image of Man is studied.
2) The single child:
   Muriel,
   Peter Brown
   Lily Tuchmann.
3) It is necessary to learn
   "The Devotion for the small things".
   Writing with toes,
   Destruction of guinea-pigs.

VI.
1) Our Ideals:
   The teachers are continuously urged
   to educate themselves.
2) The children are studied according
   to the "Image of Man" which lives
   as the high ideal before the teacher.
3) To build a village where everyone
   can live who will be unable to go
   out into the world.

VII.
1) These children are not a burden
   to the community, but an asset.
   They make Man aware of his true nature.
2) The Hydrocephalic child at Hortham Colony.
   The Mongol-child.
3) The vers from St. Johns Gospel.

Karl König's notes for a public lecture about Camphill held at the City Memorial Hall in Sheffield on May 10, 1945

Letter to Carlo Pietzner

St Christopher's School
Wraxall House, Bristol
  Sunday, November 12, 1950

Dear Carlo,

Many thanks for your letter and the report by telephone. I am very happy that Michael is getting better and when he is back in Heathcot he will get himself back together.

With this letter I am sending all the papers about the house back to you. Please instruct the office of Knight, Frank and Rutley to give you notice of larger properties (12–15 bedrooms) and particularly with at least 2 or 3 outbuildings and cottages in the grounds that can be converted and extended. I notice here in Wraxall that it is much too small and that, although they may be necessary and good, it does, however, mean a fragmentation of our energy. Curative education alone is not our sole purpose, but rather with and through those with special needs to create cultural islands. This can, however, not happen in houses as small as Wraxall.

For this reason I have spoken with Ursula [Gleed] and told her that we will not take her house in Ringwood, at least not at the moment.

We can discuss this in more detail when I am back, I only wanted you all to know how I see this at the moment.

All my love and best wishes to you and all the friends,
Your
Dr König

Tilla König at Wraxall House, Bristol

Ursula Gleed showing Karl König and Carlo Pietzner her parents' home in 1951. The estate was soon to become the Camphill Sheiling School.

The spirit like a dove: the logo of Camphill
Richard Steel

A book about the founding and the Sprit of Camphill could include much more material and various further themes, but certainly it would not be complete without a short section about the logo.

First we look briefly back to the roots and to the threads of destiny that led Karl König to become founder of such a world-wide movement. The work he had done in the Embryological Institute in Vienna was a signpost on the path of his biography with the question about the origin of the human being. This led him to anthroposophy and to Ita Wegman. 'Embryogenesis' became his theme that Wegman wanted him to teach in Arlesheim and even at the World Conference in London in 1928 which they visited together. But it was a lecture she arranged for him in Dornach that was particularly fateful. Some influential anthroposophists, in particular Marie Steiner, were not happy with the way he brought together the noble images of John the Baptist and the Sistine Madonna with 'anatomical details'. A mood began which made him partly an outcast of the Anthroposophical Society of which he had only just become a member. Nevertheless the theme never left him and the last series of lectures he gave to doctors, shortly before his death, was about this. Only later did he realise that the lecture he had given in Dornach was Whitmonday 1928, exactly 100 years after Kaspar Hauser had been released from his prison into the streets of Nuremberg, forging König's experience that Kaspar Hauser had a particular connection to his life's task. König gave many talks and seminars about embryology, also in Scotland, and his colleague Thomas Weihs continued his research.

The first Camphill Hall was built in Murtle Estate, Aberdeen in 1962. The building was extremely important for König and played a big part in the developing movement. The hall was designed with a chapel for the Sunday services at one side and a stage at the other. Above the altar there was to be a staircase that had a special function: in the various celebrations for the festivals the archangels, were to descend down this staircase into the auditorium, and for the Community Play for Christmas the Star-Bearer, the Voice of Conscience and for the three kings spoke from here. Therefore the design of the staircase was particularly important, especially the upper part of the banister, but it was not drawn exactly in the architectural plans.

The resident architect, Gabor Tallo, was probably a little hesitant as König had already overturned his planning at rather short notice because of an inspiration he had had on a journey.[8] The hall was to be finished soon, but again König was away, this time in North America, only returning on August 29. The festive opening days of the hall, for which many guests were coming from far and near, were to begin on September 20. So there would not be much time to change things radically, and the only indication Gabor had for the banister was that the form was to be 'the dove', the spirit-germ descending. It is not surprising that in these circumstances Gabor Tallo fetched Thomas Weihs as advisor. He, in turn, played down his role, describing it within a lecture he gave on Whitsunday 1967, entitled 'The Spirit Like a Dove'. The central part of the lecture is quoted here because it gives also the background to the motif and its connection to the Camphill tasks:

> I shall draw the cavity of the womb with the Fallopian tubes. These tubes go from the womb to the ovaries and they listen to the ovaries and steal from the ovaries the ovum; and the ovum thus travels through the tube and nests somewhere while all this happens. We have another organ which looks like this – and also has tubes which were discovered by an Italian biologist in the sixteenth

century. His name was Eustachi and he and Falloppio were the first to study embryonic development. The Eustachian tubes go to the middle ear and the inner ear and there you see our larynx, from which we speak; this is the organ of our word. And it has a form identical with that of the organ of conception and procreation; the female womb.

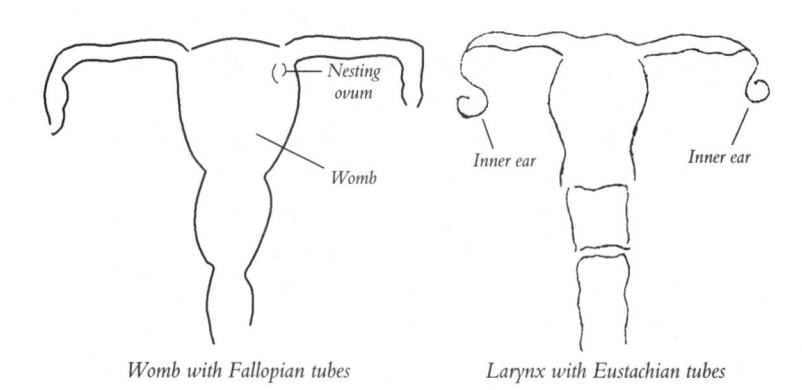

Womb with Fallopian tubes

Larynx with Eustachian tubes

It is an old occult tradition that in the far future evolution of mankind procreation will come about through speech; man in his more spiritualised phases will no longer procreate with the present organs but with the word. We can understand this if we think of the first chapter of the Gospel of John which speaks of the Word as the origin of the creation.

There is still a third organ in man which has this form – the breastbone, protecting heart and lungs, and the clavicle.

When we come to an imagination of conception, we see this form as the spirit-germ; and we see the same form as the descending dove. Gabor had no idea about the imagination of the spirit-germ when he conceived the form of our hall balcony – but as he was drawing it this

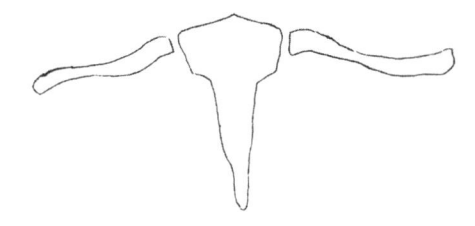

APPENDIX: THE SPIRIT LIKE A DOVE: THE LOGO OF CAMPHILL

Breastbone with clavicle

shape arose, and I just caught him and said, 'Just leave it like that.' And it is this attempt to depict the imagination of the spirit-germ, the imagination of the dove, that has now become the emblem of Camphill.

St Luke is the only one of the four Gospel writers who speaks of the Holy Spirit in connection with the Baptism in Jordan. He says: 'And the Holy Spirit descended upon him in bodily form, as a dove.'

Matthew says: 'And when Jesus was baptised, he went up immediately from the water, and behold, the heavens were opened and he saw the Spirit of God descending like a dove, and alighting on him.'

Mark says: 'And when he came up out of the water, immediately he saw the heavens opened and the Spirit descending upon him like a dove.'

And John says: 'And John [the Baptist] bore witness, "I saw the Spirit descend as a dove from heaven, and it remained on him. I myself did not know him; but he who sent me to baptise with water said to me, 'He on whom you see the Spirit descend and remain, this is he who baptises with the Holy Spirit'."'

In the Kassel lectures of 1909, *The Gospel of St John and its Relation to the Other Gospels,* Rudolf Steiner said that in the moment when the Spirit descends in the form of a dove and unites with Jesus of Nazareth is the moment of the birth of Christ: the Christ as a new

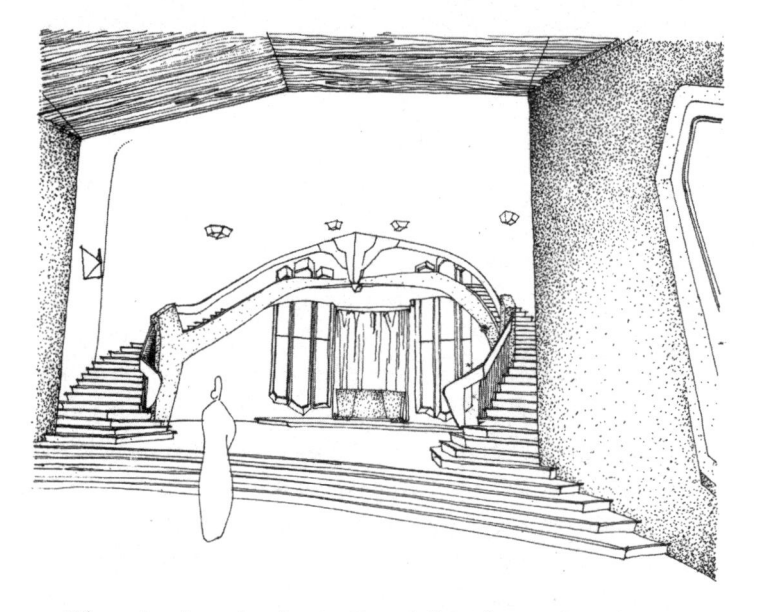

The stairs above the altar in Camphill Hall, seen from the stage

higher 'I' enters into the soul of Jesus of Nazareth and comes to birth in Jesus. He said that this Spirit which descends onto Jesus of Nazareth is the Spirit to which John points at the beginning of the first chapter – in saying, 'in the beginning was the Word'. With these words John indicates that the Spirit which descends into of Jesus of Nazareth in the form of a dove is also the Spirit described in the first chapter of Genesis with the words: 'And the Spirit of God was moving over the face of the waters. And God said, "Let there be light"; and there was light.'

Thomas Weihs went on to describe a two-way process: the Spirit of God itself descended to Jesus, and the offering Jesus made rose up to the heavens, opposite to the birth process of every human being, where the spirit-germ descends into the body at conception and the individuality descends on

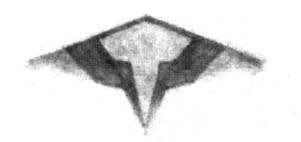

APPENDIX: THE SPIRIT LIKE A DOVE: THE LOGO OF CAMPHILL

*Sketch by Margarete Mentzel
that was used for regional versions*

Camphill Ghent
elders in community

Camphill Ghent, Inc.
2542 State Route 66 • Chatham, NY 12037
(518) 392-2760 • fax (518) 392-2762
www.camphillghent.org

Camphill Ghent, USA, present

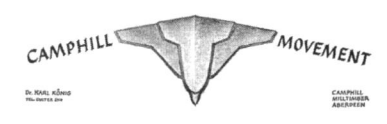

*Original letterhead
Camphill Movement*

Cresset House
A CAMPHILL RUDOLF STEINER SCHOOL
for children in need of special care
W. O. 1794

*Cresset House,
South Africa, 1966*

Karl König Institut
für Kunst, Wissenschaft und Soziales Leben e.V.

Karl König Institute, present

Camphill Community Trust

Camphill in Botswana, present

**CAMPHILL AM BODENSEE
HEIMSONDERSCHULE FÖHRENBÜHL**

Camphill School, Föhrenbühl, 1983

221

the seventeenth day. This can be seen in the image of the dove. Having descended into the situation of the conception the spirit-germ of each human being prepares the way for the individuality – the embryonic sheath. The ovum becomes surrounded by a radiating crown, which is actually called corona radiata. This can be seen as the Spirit of God hovering over the waters and saying, 'Let there be light!'

On his return on August 29, König was not only satisfied with the architectural solution but shortly afterwards declared the form to be the new logo for the letterhead of the Camphill movement. At the next Movement Council meeting it was also recommended for use in all the now evolving regions with the remark by König that it could be artistically individually interpreted for use in various circumstances and environments.

This soon led to an array of interesting variations that, however, all convey the same message, some designs changing with time or being newly created in the context of the growing diversity of Camphill. A few examples may serve to illustrate this.

Notes and Sources

Introduction

1 See Selg, *Ita Wegman and Karl König*.
2 In König, *The Child with Special Needs*, see also in the Foreword by Peter Selg.
3 This and following quotations, unless otherwise stated, are from unpublished documents of the Karl König Archive.
4 Jacques de Molay was the last Grand Master. Some sources give March 18, but March 11, 1314 is the date given by the Benedictine Bernard Grui, the contemporary historian (died 1331) of the inquisition.
5 Steiner, *The Inner Impulses of Evolution,* lecture of Sep 25, 1916.
6 The application to the Irish government is in the Appendix of *Karl König: My Task*, p. 159. The opening address at Kirkton is published in Müller-Wiedemann, *Karl König*, p. 448.
7 See Steel & Selg, *Kaspar Hauser and Karl König,* pp. 83ff.
8 Müller-Wiedemann, *Karl König,* p. 449.
9 See König, *An Inner Journey Through the Year.*
10 This 'Guide to the Anthroposophical Soul Calendar' forms the main part of König, *The Calendar of the Soul.*
11 In König *The Child with Special Needs,* p. 42.
12 See, for instance, König, *Plays for the Festivals of the Year,* Floris Books 2017.
13 The whole letter is in the Appendix, p. 214.
14 From König's address at the opening of Botton Village Community, on May 27, 1956. Published as 'The Three Great Errors' in *Camphill Villages* (Ed. Anke Weihs). Also in König, *Seeds for Social Renewal,* pp. 288–90.
15 Müller-Wiedemann, *Karl König,* pp. 480f.
16 This was the reason for naming that volume *Seeds for Social Renewal.*
17 Choruses from 'The Rock,' T.S. Eliot, *Selected Poems.*
18 These notes exactly reflect König's diary about this event quoted in König, *Kaspar Hauser and Karl König.*
19 Later he changed the title of the essay to 'The Three Stars of the Camphill Movement,' which is included in this volume.
20 See *www.karl-koenig-institute.net/subjects.htm* and *www.camphillresearch.com/*

21 'The Story of Kaspar Hauser' in König, *Kaspar Hauser and Karl König;* König, *A Christmas Story.*
22 *Ärzte-Rundbrief,* 1948/5, Stuttgart.
23 See König, *Kaspar Hauser and Karl König* for the complete text of the Requiem together with a thorough introduction by Peter Selg.

Outcasts in Scotland

Written in 1941 for the journal *Young Scotland* (Vol. 17, No. 8). It was reprinted in the journal of the Camphill movement, *The Cresset* (Vol. 15, No. 3, Christmas 1969) as 'The History of the Camphill Movement'.

The Candle on the Hill

First published in *The Cresset* (Vol. 7, No. 4, Summer 1961, a special issue for the twenty-first birthday of Camphill).
1 König was mistaken about the dates. His meeting with Ita Wegman was on November 2 and his arrival in Arlesheim was on November 19, 1927 (see *Newsletter of the Karl König Archive,* No. 9, Summer 2013).
2 Steiner, *Becoming the Archangel Michael's Companions,* lecture of Oct 15, 1922.
3 See Appendix of *Karl König: My Task,* p. 159.
4 The whole family were patients of König. The father, Antonio, was an economist and politician. His book *Un Trentennio di Lotte Politiche* (thirty years of political conflicts) describes his political views and experience, of which twenty years were in the government of Italy. In 1931 he had given up his professorship in Rome to avoid having to give an oath to Mussolini.

   König's friendship with Donna Lucia, as König called her, continued, in spite of war and relative distance. She deepened her connection to anthroposophy and discussed many questions with König by letter. After the Second World War König visited her in Italy, where she was working with disadvantaged children and children with polio. König examined children and gave advice about them. Lucia later visited Camphill on several occasions. Her last letter to him is dated just a few days before his death in March 1966. After Lucia's death in 1989 her estate went to a trust which still looks after children in the former family villa.
5 Since König's death Friedwart Bock heard that it may have been Cecil Harwood who knew the Under-Secretary of State at the Home Office who arranged for the visa. It may have been at Eugen Kolisko's request.

   Cecil Harwood knew Sir Samuel Hoare, the Home Secretary at that time, and would have been able to seek help through a personal connection. A possibility is also that Cecil Harwood's father-in-law, the politician, Lord Olivier, who certainly knew Sir Samuel, may have been a useful intermediary. Cecil Harwood (1898–1975), had studied at Oxford together with Owen Barfield and C.S. Lewis, with whom he was lifelong friends, was a teacher at Michael Hall School from

NOTES AND SOURCES

its founding as the New School in London in 1925. He was General Secretary of the Anthroposophical Society in Great Britain from 1937 until 1974, and also in that capacity it is likely that he tried to help anthroposophists from Germany and Austria gain entry to Great Britain.

Elisabeth Swann (neé Lipsker) related a that in the late 1960s Cecil Harwood once said jokingly to her that of course he was really the founder of Camphill. He was referring to his quiet help in obtaining permission for Karl König and the youth group to enter Great Britain. Being an English gentleman he would never have dreamt of mentioning it to Karl König.

6 See Appendix, p. 205, 'W.F. Macmillan and the Beginnings of Camphill'.

Three Stars, Pillars and Essentials

1 König, *Seeds for Social Renewal*, p. 263.
2 See for instance the letter König wrote to her in 1934; Selg, *Ita Wegman and Karl König*, pp. 54ff.
3 Lecture of Oct 26, 1905, published in *Beiträge zur Rudolf Steiner Gesamtausgabe*, No. 88. English translation in a (bilingual) book inspired by a Camphill conference, Roesch & Steel, *Das tun, was noch nicht da war*.
4 See his lecture 'Economics and the Spirit' given at the Camphill Economic Conference in 1984 and published to mark the centenary of his birthday in 1915 in *Camphill Correspondence* March/April and May/June 2015.
5 *Anthroposophy and the Social Question*. His remark about the lack of interest is in *Communicating Anthroposophy*, lecture of Feb 12, 1921.
6 Both included in Roesch & Steel, *Das tun, was noch nicht da war*.
7 Both in König, *The Child with Special Needs*.
8 König, *The Child with Special Needs*, pp. 41ff.

The Three Stars of the Camphill Movement

Originally published in *The Cresset*, (Vol. 6, No. 2) in 1959 entitled 'Meditations on the Camphill Movement.' In 1961 it was published together with the essay 'The Three Pillars of the Camphill Movement' in the booklet *The Camphill Movement* (see pp. 73ff, Three Stars, Pillars and Essentials, Introduction by Richard Steel).

1 Comenius was in fact invited by the English parliament to join a commission to reform public education.
2 This and subsequent quotations from Laurie, *John Amos Comenius*.
3 Young, *Comenius in England*.
4 Zinzendorf, *Wort und Weg*.
5 Podmore, *Robert Owen*.
6 Steiner, *Anthroposophy and the Social Question*, third essay.

The Three Pillars of the Camphill Movement

Originally published together with the essay 'The Three Stars of the Camphill Movement' in 1961 in *The Camphill Movement* (see pp. 73ff, Three Stars, Pillars and Essentials by Richard Steel).

1 Steiner, *The Human Spirit*, lecture of April 11, 1916, p. 99.
2 Komenský, *The Temple of Pansophia*.
3 Zinzendorf, *Wort und Weg*.
4 Matthew 28:20.
5 Steiner, *Die menschliche Seele in ihrem Zusammenhang*, lecture of April 29, 1923.
6 Steiner, *Anthroposophy and the Social Question*, beginning of the third essay.
7 Steiner, *Anthroposophy and the Social Question*, third essay.

The Three Essentials of Camphill

This essay was written as the editorial of *The Cresset*, Michaelmas 1965, commemorating 25 years of Camphill.

1 This and the following sentences set in parenthesis were cut when König revised this essay for the translation into German. He did not finish this work. See Three Stars, Pillars and Essentials by Richard Steel, p. 77.
2 Steiner, *Education for Special Needs*, lecture of June 26, 1924, p. 47.

The Birth of a Movement

Translated from the German by Tascha H. Babitch. This is the second and final part of a longer essay *(Das Werden einer Bewegung)* that König wrote in May and June 1965. The first part was published as 'Autobiographic Fragment' (in *Karl König: My Task)*; the second part was considered lost at the time. We begin this section by repeating a few paragraphs from the 'Autobiographic Fragment' in order to link on to the story of König's path into exile. As an appendix to this essay König added the application to the Irish government, 1938 (published in the Appendix of *Karl König: My Task*, p. 159), and the report by Anke Weihs of the opening ceremony of Kirkton House, Whitsunday 1939 (published in Müller-Wiedemann, *Karl König*, p. 448).

1 Steiner, *Becoming the Archangel Michael's Companions*, lecture of Oct 15, 1922, pp. 152, 156.
2 See Appendix of *Karl König: My Task*, p. 159.
3 In König's diary the name is complete: Baroness Bonnstetten. There also Baron Guy de Rothschild is named as being present at the later lunch in Paris.
4 The members of König's Youth Group are only briefly introduced, and solely in their connection to the founding situation in Kirkton. A more detailed descriptions is in the essay by John Baum in Bock, *The Builders of Camphill*, edited by Friedwart Bock, Floris Books, 2004.

5 Translation by Charles Wharton Stork, *The Lyrical Poems of Hugo Von Hofmannsthal.*
6 See Note 5 of Candle on the Hill, above.
7 Rudi Samoje was actually born on November 15, 1909, and was therefore 29 when he arrived in Kirkton and left at the age of 30. Anke Weihs also made a mistake with his age in her 'History of Camphill' (see Appendix).
8 Sandy was Alexander Innes Thompson who died 1943 in Camphill. He was one of the children in König's *Christmas Story.*
9 While composing this essay Karl König included the report of the opening celebration, written by Anke Weihs, as a second appendix. It has since been published as appendix in Müller-Wiedemann, *Karl König.*
10 See 'W.F. Macmillan and the Beginnings of Camphill,' p. 205.
11 George Fielden MacLeod, Baron MacLeod of Fuinary (June 17, 1895 – June 27, 1991) was the founder of the Iona Community. He was one of the most influential Church of Scotland ministers of the twentieth century.

Modern Community Building

Translated from German by Helen Lubin. Written for the students' journal of the University of Tübingen, Germany, and published at Easter 1966, after König had died. He had visited in 1965 for conversations with students.

1 Steiner, *Anthroposophy and the Social Question,* third essay.
2 Steiner, *Youth and the Etheric Heart,* lecture of March 20, 1921, p. 27.

Address to the Tutzinger Stern

First published for co-workers and friends of the Camphill movement for the official opening of the Camphill School Föhrenbühl on Ascension Day, 1964. Translated from the German by Helen Lubin.

On October 27, 1963, Karl König was awarded the gold medal of the Tutzinger Stern, the Bavarian section of the International Star Association for Benevolence and Humanity. This association was founded in 1954 and organised aid and emergency response training, but also awarded a medal (silver or gold) for outstanding personalities. The last gold medal before König's had been awarded to Albert Schweitzer. The Association was dissolved in 2003.

Appendix

'Fragments from the story of Camphill 1939–1940' first published in *The Cresset,* Easter 1975.

'Detailed plan for the development of a curative institute in Ireland' first publication; parts previously published in König, *My Task.*

'W.F. Macmillan and the beginnings of Camphill' first published in the first issue of *The Cresset,* Michaelmas 1954 (Vol. 1, No. 1).

1 Peter Bergel died in Botton Village on May 2, 2012, aged 83. On June 18 a special obituary appeared in *The Guardian.*

2 Rudi Samoje was actually 29. See Note 7 of 'The Birth of a Movement' above.

3 The following was added as a footnote by the editor when Anke's essay was printed in *The Cresset,* Easter 1975: 'The vision of Noah's Ark that Karl König saw resting on the peak of Bennachie has in the intervening years attained physical embodiment. Now when the floods of terror and warfare are once again covering the face of the Earth, we too must build an ark to help as many souls as we can. It is noteworthy, perhaps, that a growing international organisation, inspired by Camphill's example, has taken the name of Ark. The waters of the world storm are increasing in violence and many similar vessels will have to be built.'

4 Karl König's pictures are published in his book, *An Inner Journey Through the Year.* Peter Roth's illustrations are now in the Camphill Archive, Newton Dee, Scotland.

5 The letter about St John and Michaelmas is printed in the appendix of Müller-Wiedemann, *Karl König.*

6 At first £100 per year was agreed on as rent, and later it was bought with the accumulated rent being taken off the purchase price.

7 In fact soon an even bigger gift was to follow. One year after Mr Macmillan's death the question of what to do with the older pupils became urgent and at a parent's meeting in 1955 in Scotland, where Alistair Macmillan was now living, his aunt Peggy heard König talk about his ten-year-old hope to found a village community. She offered her family's summer residence, Botton, in Yorkshire for this purpose, and soon Botton Village began.

8 See König, *Becoming Human,* p. 39, and König, *Plays for the Festivals,* pp. 40f.

Bibliography

Bang, Jan, *Portrait of Camphill*, Floris Books 2010.
Becker, Kurt E. *Anthroposophie: Revolution von Innen*, Fischer Verlag 2018.
Bock, Friedwart (ed.) *The Builders of Camphill*, Floris Books 2004.
Buber, Martin, *I and Thou*, Scribner Classics, 2000.
Comenius, John Amos, *Pandromus Pansophiae* or *Pansophici Libri Delineatio*, Oxford 1637, translated into English, published under Komenský (Comenius' Czech name), *The Temple of Pansophia*, London *c*. 1912.
Eliot, T.S. *Selected Poems*, Macmillan, UK 1935.
König, Karl, *Becoming Human: A Social Task*, Floris Books 2011.
—, *The Calendar of the Soul*, Floris Books 2009.
—, *The Child with Special Needs*, Floris Books 2009.
—, *A Christmas Story*, Camphill Books 1995.
—, *History of the Bible Evening*, Aberdeen University Press 1953.
—, *An Inner Journey Through the Year*, Floris Books 2009.
—, *Karl König: My Task*, Floris Books 2008.
—, *Kaspar Hauser and Karl König*, Floris Books 2012.
—, *Plays for the Festivals of the Year*, Floris Books 2017.
—, *Seeds for Social Renewal*, Floris Books 2009.
Laurie, S.S. *John Amos Comenius*, Cambridge 1887.
Luxford, Michael and Jane, *A Sense for Community: The Camphill Movement*, Directions for Change 2003.
Müller-Wiedemann, Hans, *Karl König: A Central-European Biography of the Twentieth Century*, Camphill Books, 1996.
Pietzner, Cornelius, *A Candle on the Hill*, Floris Books 1999.
Podmore, Frank, *Robert Owen*, 2 vols. London 1906.
Roesch, Ulrich & Richard Steel, *Das tun, was noch nicht da war / We Create the Social Conditions*, Verlag am Goetheanum, Switzerland 2006.
Selg, Peter, *Ita Wegman and Karl König*. Floris Books 2008.
Stork, Charles Wharton, *The Lyrical Poems of Hugo Von Hofmannsthal*, Yale University, 1918.
Steiner, Rudolf, *Anthroposophy and the Social Question*, Mercury Press, USA 1982.
—, *Becoming the Archangel Michael's Companions: Rudolf Steiner's Challenge to the Younger Generation* (CW 217) Steinerbooks, USA 2006.
—, *The Bridge between Universal Spirituality and the Physical Constitution of Man* (CW 202) Anthroposophic Press, USA 1979.

—, *Communicating Anthroposophy: the Course for Speakers to Promote the Idea of Threefolding* (CW 338) Steinerbooks, USA 2015.
—, *Education for Special Needs: the Curative Education Course* (CW 317) Rudolf Steiner Press, UK 1998.
—, *The Gospel of St John and its Relation to the Other Gospels* (CW 112) Anthroposophic Press, USA 1982.
—, *The Human Spirit: Past and Present, Occult Fraternities and the Mystery of Golgotha* (CW 167) Rudolf Steiner Press, UK 2016.
—, *The Inner Impulses of Evolution: the Mexican Mysteries and the Knights Templar* (CW 171) Anthroposophic Press, USA 1984.
—, *Man's Being, his Destiny and World Evolution* (CW 226) Anthroposophic Press, USA 1984.
—, *Die menschliche Seele in ihrem Zusammenhang mit göttlich-geistigen Individualitäten* (GA 224) Rudolf Steiner Verlag, Switzerland 1983.
—, *Spiritual Science as a Foundation for Social Forms* (CW 199) Anthroposophic Press, USA 1986.
—, *Youth and the Etheric Heart: Rudolf Steiner Speaks to the Younger Generation* (CW 217a) SteinerBooks, USA 2007.
Weihs, Anke, *History of the Camphill Community Since 1954*, Camphill Press, 1975.
— (ed.), *The Camphill Movement*, a special issue of *The Cresset*.
— (ed.), *Camphill Villages*, Camphill Press 1989.
Weihs, Thomas, *Embryogenesis in Myth and Science*, Floris Books 1996.
Young, R. Fitzgibbon, *Comenius in England*, Humphrey Milford, London 1932.
Zinzendorf, *Wort und Weg*, Hanau 1958.

Index

Adams, George 56
Advent garden 50f
Amann, Willi 152
Andrian, Leopold Baron 145
Anschluss of Austria 12
Anthroposophical Society,
 problems of the 8
Arandora Star 201
Aristotle 135
Arlesheim 49
Arnim, Georg von 33, 77f

Bang, Jan 72
Bangor, monastery of 101
Baum, Alex 151, 164, 191, 201
Bennachie 158, 187
Bergel, Peter 160f, 163, 186
Bible Evening 17, 79, 116–18, 126, 203
Bittleston, Kalmia 188
Blau, Trude 151, 163, 191, 194f, 197
Blitz, Marie 152, 163, 184, 194f, 197
Blum, Mrs 188
Bock, Emil 15
Bonnet, Georges 148
Botton 24, 32
— Village 186
Brachenreuthe 32
Brandstädter, Rosa 152
Brown, Robert Dods 168
Bucknall, Morwenna 74
Campbell, J. Downie 169, 201

Camphill
— Hall 36, 216
— House 11, 16, 45, 68, 193–95, 205f
— movement 30, 108, 109
— Movement Council 34
Cappel, Professor 159
Christian Community, The 18
Christophorus, Huize 32
college meetings 79, 112–14, 126
Comenius, John Amos 96f, 99f, 105, 107, 110f, 114
Cyprus 64, 143

Dawn Farm 32
Doldinger, Friedrich 15
Donna Lucia *see* Marco, Lucia de Viti de
Downingtown School 32

Eliot, T.S. 29
embryogenesis 216
embryology 9
Engel, Hans-Heinrich 36
equality 137
Eustachian tubes 218

Fallopian tubes 218
Fama Fraternitatis 95
Föhrenbühl 26–28
Förster, Hanna and Hedda 152
fraternity 137

231

French Revolution 127
Frischauer, Hugo 152
fundamental social law 106, 122, 126, 174

Gerstler, Sally *see* Lipsker, Barbara
Gladstone, Dr 18, 30
Gleed, Ursula 214f
Glencraig School 32
Goetheanum 8f, 52
Grange 32

Hart, Edith Tudor 19
Hauser, Kaspar 30f, 38, 188, 216
Heathcot House 162
Heidenreich, Alfred 18
Herrnhut Brotherhood 98, 101
Hitler, Adolf 58
Hofmannsthal, Hugo von 145
Houghton, Mr and Mrs 65f, 68, 153–55, 159, 162f, 165, 167, 183, 188, 192
Hubermann, Bronislav 146

internment 170, 194, 202, 206
Irish Republic 64, 143
Isle of Man 43, 69, 198

James I 92
Jeetze, Herr and Frau von 54

Kirkton House 42, 66–69, 154f, 158, 162, 165, 183, 186–88, 190, 192–95
Knights Templar 11f
Kokoschka, Oskar 150
Kolisko, Eugen 65, 156f, 165f, 168
König
— children 163
—, Karl 183, 186f, 199, 202, 204

—, Mathilde (née Maasberg) 14f, 52–55, 57, 66f, 156, 183f, 186, 194–97, 215
—, Renate 189
Kristallnacht 147

Lehenhof 28
Lehrs, Ernst 199
Leney
—, Robert 163
—, Robin 161
liberty 137
Lindenberg, Christof-Andreas 73
Lipsker, Barbara 151, 204
Lohmann, Ruth 33
Luxford, Michael and Jane 72

Macanna, Robert Clephane 67
MacLeod, George 167f, 196
Macmillan
—, Alistair 192
—, Peggy 167
—, W.F. 68, 167, 192, 194, 205–8
Mahler, Gustav 79
Marco
—, Etta de Viti de 64, 144
—, Lucia de Viti de 64–66, 144, 148, 156
Marti, Ernst 146
Meisel
—, Friedel 152
—, Hermann 152
Memorandum
—, First 18, 30
—, Second 23, 83
—, Third 78
Molay, Jakob von 141f
Moravian-Bohemian Brotherhood 53, 97, 101
Müller-Wiedemann, Hans 36, 76, 145

Musil, Robert 150
Nederhoed, Anke *see* Weihs, Anke
New Lanark 120
Newton Dee 32, 207f
Noah's Ark 158, 187
Nuremberg Laws 58

Owen, Robert 74, 84, 96, 98f, 102–4, 106f, 119f, 124

pansophia 110
pansophic 99
Pestalozzi 173
Pietzner
—, Carlo 36, 62, 82, 85, 150, 157, 164, 202, 214f
—, Cornelius 72
Pilgramshain 9, 15, 56, 59
Pini, Sabine 152

Ringwood 32
Robertson, Fyfe 20
Roth
—, Alix 30, 62, 67, 150, 157, 183, 194–97
—, Emil 44, 152f, 188
—, Peter 18, 36, 62, 66f, 149f, 157, 183, 189, 198, 202

Samoje, Rudi 161, 187
Sauerwein, Jules 148
Schauder
—, Hans 151f, 164, 166, 202f
—, Lisl (née Schwalb) 151, 159, 166, 194
Schubert, Karl 191
Sheffield 212
Sheiling School 215
Somervell, Jonty 163
Sonnenhof 49

South Africa 71
Starhemberg, Countess 148
Steiner
—, Marie 216
—, Rudolf 9, 11, 84, 105f, 179
Stein, Walter-Johannes 59
Strohschein, Albrecht 54, 56
Sucher, Willi 199
Sunday Service for children 117f, 188

Tallo, Gabor 217
Thompson, Sandy 161, 163
Thornbury 32
tradition 79
Tutzinger Stern 179

United States 82

village community 24f, 28f

Waldorf School 85, 169
Wegman, Ita 8f, 37, 48, 55f, 65, 145f, 192
Weihs
—, Anke (née Nederhoed) 30, 40, 67, 73, 75, 149, 197
—, Thomas 36, 62, 149–51, 164, 191, 198, 202f, 216f, 220
Weissberg, Eduard 152
Werfel-Mahler, Alma 148
Wiesenthal, Grete 149
work, paid 77, 80
Wraxall House 215

youth group 62

Zinzendorf, Ludwig Count 15, 17, 96–98, 100–102, 105, 107, 114f, 118
Zuckmayer, Carl 145

More books from the Karl König Archive

Plays for the Festivals of the Year

Karl König

Karl König's plays for the festivals of the year are arguably his most original creations. Written to be performed in Camphill communities, they reflect a deep understanding of the Christian festivals.

This is the first time that the original texts of all of his plays have been published together. The book includes performance photographs as well as an introduction and commentary by series editor Richard Steel.

Volume 17

florisbooks.co.uk

Seeds for Social Renewal
The Camphill Village Conferences

Karl König

"His lectures are easily accessible and inspiring...
containing advice that can be lived with,
discussed and practised immediately."
– *Camphill Correspondence*

Seeds for Social Renewal explores the human being and social life, the individual and community. These lectures are based on König's own experiences in building up Camphill communities and are important for both the work in Camphill, as well as more broadly in the field of social therapy and beyond.

Volume 5

florisbooks.co.uk

The Child with Special Needs
Letters and Essays on Curative Education

Karl König

The Child with Special Needs is a fascinating collection of Karl König's letters and essays in which he considers and discusses the fundamentals of special needs education.

Volume 4

florisbooks.co.uk

Communities for Tomorrow

Edited by Richard Steel

"This book gives tremendous scope of interest, insight and involvement. It gives a strong taste of the mission of Camphill and the vision Karl König had."
– *Camphill Correspondence*

Communities for Tomorrow is an anthology compiled of contributions from the Community Building conference which took place at the Goetheanum in 2009. Each article considers how can we connect with one another and build successful communities, whilst also cultivating a healthy individuality.

Volume 9

florisbooks.co.uk

Karl König: My Task
Autobiography and Biographies

Karl König & Peter Selg

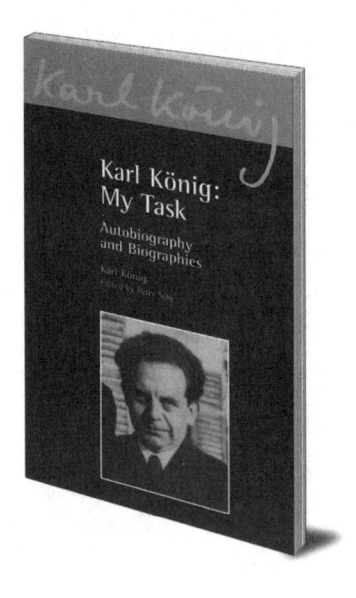

Karl König: My Task is an inspiring introduction to König's remarkable life and work. This book combines König's autobiographical fragment and an essay by Peter Selg with two selected reminiscences written by König's colleagues Anke Weihs and Hans-Heinrich Engel.

Volume 1

florisbooks.co.uk

Floris Books

For news on all our **latest books**,
and to receive **exclusive discounts**,
join our mailing list at:

florisbooks.co.uk

Plus subscribers get a FREE book
with every online order!

We will never pass your details to anyone else.

Karl König's collected works are being published in English by Floris Books and in German by Verlag Freies Geistesleben. They are issued by the Karl König Archive in co-operation with the Ita Wegman Institute for Basic Research into Anthroposophy. They encompass the entire, wide-ranging literary estate of Karl König, including his books, essays, manuscripts, lectures, diaries, notebooks, his extensive correspondence and his artistic works, across twelve subjects.

Karl König Archive subjects

Medicine and study of the human being
Curative education and social therapy
Psychology and education
Agriculture and science
Social questions
The Camphill movement
Christianity and the festivals
Anthroposophy
Spiritual development
History and biographies
Artistic and literary works
Karl König's biography

Karl König Archive
www.karl-koenig-archive.net
kk.archive@camphill.net

Research into Anthroposophy
www.wegmaninstitut.ch
koenigarchiv@wegmaninstitut.ch

Ita Wegman Institute for Basic